Day Trading for Beginners 2020:

The Ultimate Penny Stocks, Options and Psychology Swing Strategies For a Living Like a Rich Dad, Using The Tools, Tactics, Money Management, Discipline and Bases.

ROBERT ZONE

Table of Contents

Introduction

Chapter 1 Basics of Day Trading & Qualities of a Day Trader

Chapter 2 Concepts of Day Trading

Chapter 3 How Day Trading Works

Chapter 4 How to Reduce Your Risks When Day Trading

Chapter 5 Finding and Picking Stocks and Trading Strategies

Chapter 6 Day Trading Tools

Chapter 7 Understanding Trading Orders

Chapter 8 Money Management

Chapter 9 Dos and Don'ts

Chapter 10 Managing Risk in Trading and the Role of Journaling

Conclusion

© **Copyright 2019 - All rights reserved.**

The content contained within this book may not be reproduced, duplicated or transmitted without direct written permission from the author or the publisher.

Under no circumstances will any blame or legal responsibility be held against the publisher, or author, for any damages, reparation, or monetary loss due to the information contained within this book. Either directly or indirectly.

Legal Notice:

This book is copyright protected. This book is only for personal use. You cannot amend, distribute, sell, use, quote or paraphrase any part, or the content within this book, without the consent of the author or publisher.

Disclaimer Notice:

Please note the information contained within this document is for educational and entertainment purposes only. All effort has been executed to present accurate, up to date, and reliable, complete information. No warranties of any kind are declared or implied. Readers acknowledge that the author is not engaging in the rendering of legal, financial, medical or professional advice. The content within this book has been derived from various sources. Please consult a licensed professional before attempting any techniques outlined in this book.

By reading this document, the reader agrees that under no circumstances is the author responsible for any losses, direct or indirect, which are incurred as a result of the use of information contained within this document, including, but not limited to, — errors, omissions, or inaccuracies.

Introduction

The stock market is a vast place and there are millions of trades that take place all over the world, within a single day. There are both buyers and sellers in the market and they will all have the same motive in mind; to increase their wealth potential.

Of all these trades, not everything will be of the same nature. Some will be long-term investments and some short. Long-term investments refer to those that are held for a long period of time. They are preferred by those who are not in a hurry to make money. Short-term investments on the other hand are those that are liquidated within a short period of time. They are not meant to be held for a long time, as the owners will be interested in disposing them off early.

Short-term investments can be of many types based on the time that they are held. Some can be held for a month, some for a week and some will be disposed off on the same day. This book will focus on the last option.

Better known as Intraday trading, day trading is one of the most preferred ways to trade in the stock market. Preferred mostly by those willing to part with their investment within a single day and realize a profit, or loss, from.

Intraday traders are interested in realizing a profit by capitalizing on the difference in the rates of these securities as opposed to long-term investors who will be in it for the Dividends.

Intraday trading has the capacity to help you attain a big leverage, as the rate of return on your investments can be quite high. However, it can also go the other way and cause you to lose out on a lot of money owing to poor investments. It is up to you to make the right choices and invest your money wisely.

You have to understand that the stock market is a very volatile place and anything can happen within a matter of a few seconds. You have to be prepared for anything that it throws at you. In order to prepare for it, you have to make use of risk capital. Risk capital refers to money that you are willing to risk. You have to convince yourself that even if you lose the money that you have invested then it will not be a big deal for you. For that, you have to make use of your own money and not borrow from anyone, as you will start feeling guilty about investing it. Decide on a set number and invest it.

You have to conduct a thorough research on the market before investing in it. Don't think you will learn as you go. That is only possible if you at least know the basics. You have to remain interested in gathering information that is crucial for your investments and it will only come about if you put in some hard work towards it. Nobody is asking you to stay up and go through thick texts books. All you have to do is go through books and websites and gather enough information to help you get started on the right foot.

Chapter 1   Basics of Day Trading & Qualities of a Day Trader

Before the invention of online trading platforms, people could only engage in stock market trading through brokerage firms, financial institutions, and other trading houses. As more inventions related to the internet were made, it became easy for individual traders to invest in the stock market. One way you can make money on the stock market is through day trading.

Day trading is one technique that can help you gain a lot of income if used properly. However, it becomes a challenge for those who have little information or those who lack the right trading strategies. Sometimes, even the most experienced traders end up losing a fortune because of inadequate knowledge and planning.

Definition

Day trading refers to a technique of stock trading that involves buying and selling of security or assets within a single day. Although day trading takes place in most marketplaces, it is more common in forex and stock trading platforms. For you to succeed in this kind of trade, you must have enough capital. The main goal is to leverage the profit on every slight price movement.

When day trading, you must ensure that each position you open closes by the end of the same day. This means that you cannot hold a position overnight. Instead, you must close the position in the evening and reopen it the next day. It is the opposite of long-term trading where you purchase stock, hold it for some time then sell it off at a profit. That is why day trading is not considered as a form of investment.

Individuals who engage in this kind of trade are known as day traders. As a day trader, you must master how prices move in the marketplace. This is important if you want to make a profit from each short term price movement. A trader can make an unlimited number of trades within a single day. However, beginners can limit themselves to one or a few trades depending on the amount of capital and time available. If a trade does not seem quite profiting at the end of the day, you may decide to let it continue to the next day. However, you will be required to pay some fee to your broker for this to happen.

How long each transaction lasts depends on the trader. Some complete trades in a matter of seconds or minutes while others take several hours. Traders who purchase and sell multiple times within the same day usually end up with high-profit volumes. Some traders prefer selling their stock as soon as a good profit has been realized. Others prefer to wait until the close of the day to end their positions.

Qualities of a Good Day Trader

Day traders who engage in the business as a career always seek to improve their skills each day. They possess in-depth knowledge of the market as well as the strategies required to make good cash from the market. So, who is the right person to engage in day trading? Let us look at some of the characteristics one should possess.

1. *Market Experience* – if you happen to engage in day trading without the requisite knowledge of the market, you may lose all your capital. You must be good at reading charts and carrying out technical analysis of the prices and market trends. You must also be able to carry out all the due diligence required to ensure you maximize the profits you realize from the trade.

2. *Adequate capital* – like any other trade, you need sufficient amounts of money to day trade. You must understand that this should be risk capital that you are ready to lose in case the market does not perform in your favor. Preparing yourself this way will save you the emotional torture associated with loss of cash in the trade. You must invest large

capitals if you want to make more significant returns.

3. *A good strategy* – several strategies are involved in day trading. You need these strategies to stay ahead of other traders on the market. Before you start trading, you must understand how to apply these strategies in your transactions. When used correctly, these strategies ensure more consistent returns and fewer losses.

4. *Discipline* – it is essential to be disciplined as a day trader. Without discipline, it becomes difficult to record any successful transactions. Day trading depends on the volatility of stock prices. Traders are often interested in stocks whose price changes a lot in the course of the day. However, if you are not disciplined enough in the way you select your shares, you may end up losing a lot despite the substantial price changes.

This trait is particularly crucial because the stock market has uncountable trading opportunities. You may decide to trade on several industries, products, and assets, but the truth is – not all these opportunities are good for making a profit.

If you are disciplined enough, you will spend time analyzing opportunities before investing in them. You will also open and close trades at the right time, and this will ensure that you minimize losses.

5. *Patience* – day trading involves a certain level of waiting. You need to time when to enter the market and when to exit. Getting into the market blindly always results in a lot of problems. You must be patient enough to get into trades in good time.

Besides being patient, you also need to adapt to the changes taking place in the market. For instance, how a market appears at the beginning of the day is not the same way it will be at midday. You must be able to adjust your strategies to accommodate market changes accordingly.

Most successful day traders always seek to acquire these characteristics as a way of improving their business. Doing this requires a high level of mental as well as financial flexibility. You must be thick-skinned enough to risk your capital and accept any losses that come along. Remember, the main difference between successful and unsuccessful day traders lies in the profits. More profits depict you as a successful trader while less profits display you as one that is on the losing end. However, losing trades should not make you focus less because even professional day traders started by losing.

Chapter 2   Concepts of Day Trading

Traditionally, most of the people who used to trade in the stock market were those who work in brokerages, trading houses, and financial institution. Thanks to the influx of technology and the internet, there has been a rise in online trading places. Brokers have taken advantage of that and individuals are able to play the games online. This is also the reason why many people are aware of day trading. This has turned out to be a rising and lucrative business. The secret is to make sure that you completely understand what it entails, practice and learn more. For the newbies, it can be a little bit challenging. You do not need to worry since with the right strategy, approach and plan you are bound to succeed. What you should know is that even the most experienced day traders have their failures and a bad day. First, you need to know how day trading works.

How Does Day Trading Work?

What you should know is that day trading is not an investment. It involves purchasing an asset stake hopefully to make a profit over a set period. The length of time to anticipate the profit is subjective. This is because most investors are always open to the idea of holding their assets for many years, which can end up to decades. The secret is to be aware of the industry you are investing in. Always look for firms that are known to make great profit margins. They are the best since your profitability and great returns are guaranteed. Look for firms that are debt-free, have a strong product line, and do not have any pending lawsuits.

Day traders will buy and sell financial securities within a day. Traders will look for different sources of funds to buy the securities. Most of them will borrow funds and buy when the security prices are lower anticipating them to rise later in the day. The basic principle is to always buy when the cost is low and sell when it is high. That is where you will get the best profit margins. This s always managed at a compressed time limit.

An example is when a trader buys around 500 shares at 9:00 am. After 30 minutes, the price goes up, and he decides to sell. He will end up making a profit for that day less the commission chargeable and any applicable taxes. You need to know that when you sell a stock or investment that you have owned for less than a year. It is normally taxed against your personal gains. They are taxed at 35% as opposed to the long-term ones that are taxed at around 20%. It is evident that when day trading, you should put into consideration the taxation concept.

The beauty of day trading is that you have the ability to have at least 25 trades per day. The profit margin will increase based on the number of trades. Day traders always limit their risks, by not owning their stock overnight to avoid drastic price changes. The main reason could be market volatility hence the need for immediate response. Day traders will act quickly and make fast decisions, unlike other traders who will take time to make any decision.

What does a Day Trader do?

Day trader's typical day involves participating in financial markets purchasing and disposing of stocks, forex, and other securities. Their work also involves closing positions in order to make small and regular profits. There are different types of traders. The small-scale ones, the independent ones with their home space, and the ones based in institutions. Apart from trading, they also manage and maintain different markets and do research. They also do an analysis of financial notes based on securities and exchange information with the other traders.

This type of trading is considered to be on the fast lane and requires someone who can handle a lot of challenges and stress. You will need a deep and clear understanding of how the market works. You will also need to possess the required trading skills to be successful. One of the skills includes the ability to analyze different price charts.

A day trader always starts its day before the financial markets open. They will check all the financial information to help in economic development, analytical reports, market data, and any political news. They also check and do an analysis of the technical indicators and any results from the trading. The information they rely upon is from their subscription and analyst. This information is crucial and helps in decision-making.

The other duty for a day trader is to check any confirmations from trading. The confirmation is from the trading from the previous day. Then they check any activity notes and the overnight position that they hold. In case there are any errors, they need to be fixed immediately. Since all the charges are billed to the trader.

Then they will ensure that the trades have been successfully settled. The next thing will be to check the cash that the got and the profit in their trading account. What they confirm is if there is a purchase that was not sent to their accounts. Or a third party to a sale who has not paid for the security. They need to immediately address that since it is bound to affect their trading ability.

The most important part of a trader's life is when the market opens. The trader will put all the orders in the open that is entirely dependent on their style and plans. Then they will enter follow-ups on the trades that they intend to sell or buy. They spend the most part of the day doing analysis. Analyzing financial reports and charts with price movements.

An hour before the market closes; the trader will then close all the positions before leaving for the day. This is to ensure that there are no overnight risks.

Making a profit is any trader's goal. When they are private traders, they will bank all the profit. For the employed ones, they earn a percentage of the gains since they trade under customers' accounts. When there is a loss, nothing is paid. In fact, they need to refund the cash advances to the trading account.

Other duties of a day trader include doing market analysis and observation. Trading strategies formulation and completing a trade with brokers. They ensure that they sell all assets by the close of the day and have the investment as cash and profits. They also cut losses when there is a failure in investment. They are required to complete tax returns and do transaction recording.

Techniques Used in Day Trading

You need to have the best techniques when it comes to trading. Day trading can be considered simple or complicated based on the techniques and approaches that you use. Ensure that you are familiar with the concept and all that it entails. The best techniques are the ones that will help in maximizing profit and minimize price movements. In order to have effective approaches, you will need to depend on in-depth analysis, use price charts, and price indicators. The patterns will help in predicting price changes in the future.

This chapter will illustrate the best strategies and techniques to adopt that will help all traders on a different level; from beginners to experts. You will be able to know how to position yourself and know about the resources that are useful. The important thing to note is ensuring that you pick a technique that will perfectly fit with your preference, requirements, and style.

When you are starting out in the world of trading, do not be n a hurry to master all the technical terms and processes. Starts with the basics first; do not think that having a complicated technique is what will make you successful. You should know that the simpler your plan is the more effective it will be.

- You need to understand all the components of money management. You need to know the amount of money you are ready to risk as your capital. Note that it is not advisable to put down anything above 2% of your capital for each trade. Ensure that you are aware that you are also bound to make losses.

- Ensure you know how to manage your time. Day trading will need you to input a lot of your time. And you should also know how to strike a balance between your professional and personal life. Do not expect to allocate like an hour or two, and expect to have great returns. Be attentive in monitoring the financial markets and looking for new trading chances.

- Start small, do not be in a hurry to invest a lot of capital. Learn a lot, master the skill then invest more. You can start with at least 3 stocks daily. It is considered wise to start with fewer stocks and make great returns that investing in more and not gaining anything.

- The only way to understand the market and master it is by learning a lot. You need to keep yourself informed on what is happening. Be updated on what is happening, any news or occasions. Ensure you know about asset implications especially when there is a shift in economic policies.

- Be consistent with your trading. Deliver work with the same morale and spirit. Depend on logical facts and a strategic plan. Always ensure that your timing is always right. This is because when the market opens, it becomes volatile. Experts will be able to read the patterns, you should be able to bide the time. You can hold on in the first minutes of trading.

There are several components that each trader is s meant to know. Be it a beginner or experienced, you should master the components.

Volatility: This component will illustrate the potential gain in each trade. Great volatility means greater gains or losses.

Liquidity: This component makes a trader enter and exit the trading period and still manage a stable and attractive price.

Volume: Volume is a component that will indicate the number of times a stock has been traded over a certain time. It is commonly known as the average daily trading volume. When the volume is high, it indicates higher gains or interest in the trade. When the volume increases, it means that there is a change in price.

What is the Market to Day Trade?

There are three different markets for day trading. They are forex, futures, and stock market. Most people are aware of the stock market and not future and forex.

Stock Market: When people think of day trading, stock market comes into their mind first. It is considered the best when it comes to buying and selling company shares. And you'll need to exit all positions by the close of the trading period. There is a requirement to hold at least $25k in your account, anything less will not be accepted in day trading. The required capital to start is $30k.

Future Market: This is another market for day trading. This is where there is an agreement between a seller and a buyer. They agree to sell or buy at an agreed amount at a certain time. Traders make their gains from price fluctuations. This is from the difference computed between what is bought or sold and when the position closes. For this market, you do not need too much capital, a minimum of $3500 and a maximum of $5k is enough to start. The opening hours vary, you need to be careful and ensure that before the trade closes, you are out. You need to consider access to the future market and know of the requirements. Usually, there is a limit on the minimum balance; it is set at $2k.

Forex Market: This is considered a common and accessible market; it trades for 24 hours in a day. They are allowed to start with a minimum capital of around $100, what is recommended is at least $500 to start with. They only deal with one currency and that could be a limitation when it comes to the investment currency. There are also specifications and requirements for this trading platform. As a trader, you need to be careful of the platform that you choose, ensure it is something that fits your preferences and needs. There are demo accounts that can be used to practice and apply the techniques you have learned.

Several factors will affect your choice for a trading market. They include your financial position, the trading technique that, interests and personality. An example is when you want to start trading and your capital is below $25k. You will not be able to trade unless you continue saving up. When your capital is adequate, you can choose any of the trading markets listed above. You need to know that there are other techniques that will work in one market and not the other.

And others will work in a certain time and others not. Always When you have a technique to adopt, choose one market and stick to that. When you are new to day trading, do not flip between markets but maintain a market. You are allowed to shift between trades based on the time you are trading.

All three markets are considered great. You will choose a market based on your preference and interest. However, it is recommended to stick to one market, as you know more about the others.

What is the Expected Monthly Income from Day Trading?

Most people start day trading for different reasons. To some it is just a lifestyle, others business and others love the challenge. The amount of money that day traders make vary, some will lose capital will others will use it to gain more income. How the trader makes their income is influenced by the approach they use and how they manage their risk. The secret to more income is to have a better approach, ensure you are able to manage your risk and work hard.

Most traders will ensure that their risk is small, equivalent to at least 1 % of the capital they use to trade in with. If you are trading with stock worth $3000, ensure that your risk is not more than $30.

The strategy that is used in trading is normally in two categories: the win rate and the profit that is relative to losses. The win rate is described as the number of times a trader wins. And then you need to divide that by a number of trades. For instance, when a strategy wins at 60 trades from 100 trades. That will be at 60%. Having a high win rate is every trader's wish. But that will not make you profitable if your wins are high, but fewer winners that are not considered profitable. The win rate is expected to be at least 50%. And the reward to risk ratio is a factor that needs to be considered. In any given time, traders will expect to have bigger winners than losers.

Even though day trading is the most common and known, it also requires more capital investment. Let's assume a day trader starts their trading at $40k, and you use a 4:1 ratio. It will give a buying power of $160k (4 x $40k), ensure you have a reward to risk ratio is 1.5:1. This will be in terms of $0.15 as winning trades and $0.10 as losing trades.

This means that the maximum loss you can encounter is $400, which is 1% of $30k. To achieve that, you will need to trade with stocks that have high volatility and volume.

When you choose a good strategy in your trading, you are guaranteed 50% of the profit. So if you have 5 trades daily, and you trade 20 days per month; that is an equivalent of 100 trades monthly. So that will be computed as 50 x $0.15 x 4000 = $30,000. And if the other half was a loss, that will be 50 x $0.10 x 4000 = $20,000. So your gain will be $10,000 and you'll need to deduct commission chargeable and some other fees.

Another example is when the trade cost is $10, the commission will be 100 trades by $10= $1000. Your take-home will be $10,000 - $1000 = $9,000 per month.

Day Trading Hardware Requirements

For you to be a successful day trader there are several tools of the trade that are required. You might already possess some of them. Modern trading is mostly done online, and you will be able to view and access financial markets on the internet and have access to the trades. Therefore, the first equipment you will need is s a laptop or a computer. Then organize how you will be accessing your internet. There will come a time when you will need to call your broker for clarification or update. At that point, you will need a phone to be able to do that.

You will also need access to brokerage, market data in real-time, and chart for trading. All this will enable you to run your trades effectively and smoothly. Day trading needs advance and updated technology. So when getting a laptop or computer ensure you get one with enough memory and a faster processor to avoid any lagging or crashing. Ensure that the machine s faster when it comes to loading information. If you get that your workload is constantly increasing, you can invest in two desktops.

When you have a problem with your internet, the only way you can communicate with your brokers will be via a phone call. Ensure you invest in a phone or landline for trading purposes. As a backup tip, ensure you program your broker's number on your phone. So that when you do not have access to the internet or your computer breaks down, you can access their number.

To succeed in day trading, you will need a broker; a company that helps in the facilitation of the trades. Day traders do a lot of trades on a daily basis, this is why they need a broker who will charge low commissions and the best trading software. There are brokers that are known from banks, but the problem is they charge high commission and do not have solutions tailor-made for day traders. Day traders are advised to always seek services of brokers who are small scale and regulated. Make sure if you choose software that is compatible with the brokers.

You will need to have access to accurate financial information and data. Most of them are derived from price movements and changes from the assets and markets they are trading in. You'll need to request the information that you need from the broker. You will get some brokers giving information free but in return, the commission charges are high. The basic requirements are a quick and reliable laptop or desktop, a working telephone, and software for trading. You should consider getting a smartphone that can use backup internet. Plan for reliable and fast internet connectivity and find a broker who is regulated. One who charges commissions that are low and will provide trading software. The last thing will be to subscribe to market information of your choice based on the trading market.

Day Trading Software Requirements

The trading charts require a processor and a memory component; they should be of high speed and updated. Do not go for software that will make your screen to freeze once you become busy analyzing your trades. Look for internet connectivity that is fast enough to help in loading web pages. If that is not possible, consider your internet slow to do any day trading. When there are price movements and changes, you will be getting thousands of information to your computer. The streaming is done per second. Therefore, that means it is a lot of data per hour for a day.

When it is too slow to do all that, you will have a lag experience. Lag simply means, receiving old data instead of new. You will have data backlog and not able to see any current prices. Take a test from all the internet providers before making a choice.

Always consider having internet access with a backup plan. This will help when there is an internet outage, you will still be able to access the internet. This can be done easily using a smartphone, via hot spot or mobile data. The backup plan should be outsourced from a company different from the internet provider. So that when the internet connectivity goes done, it will not affect the backup plan.

Chapter 3   How Day Trading Works

There was a time when the only people able to trade in financial markets were those working for trading houses, brokerages, and financial institutions. The rise of the internet, however, made things easier for individual traders to get in on the action. Day Trading, in particular, can be a very profitable career, as long as one goes about it in the right way.

However, it can be quite challenging for new traders, especially those who lack a good strategy. Furthermore, even the most experienced day traders hit rough patches occasionally. As stated earlier, Day Trading is the purchase and sale of an asset within a single trading day. It can happen in any marketplace, but it is more common in the stock and forex markets.

Day traders use short-term trading strategies and a high level of leverage to take advantage of small price movements in highly liquid currencies or stocks. Experienced day traders have their finger on events that lead to short-term price movements, such as the news, corporate earnings, economic statistics, and interest rates, which are subject to market psychology and market expectations.

When the market exceeds or fails to meet those expectations, it causes unexpected, significant moves that can benefit attuned day traders. However, venturing into this line of business is not a decision prospective day trader should take lightly. It is possible for day traders to make a comfortable living trading for a few hours each day.

However, for new traders, this kind of success takes time. Think like several months or more than a year. For most day traders, the first year is quite tough. It is full of numerous wins and losses, which can stretch anyone's nerves to the limit. Therefore, a day trader's first realistic goal should be to hold on to his/her trading capital.

Volatility is the name of the game when it comes to Day Trading. Traders rely on a market or stock's fluctuations to make money. They prefer stocks that bounce around several times a day, but do not care about the reason for those price fluctuations. Day traders will also go for stocks with high liquidity, which will allow them to enter and exit positions without affecting the price of the stock.

Day traders might short sell a stock if its price is decreasing or purchase if it is increasing. Actually, they might trade it several times in a day, purchasing it and short-selling it a number of times, based on the changing market sentiment. In spite of the trading strategy used, their wish is for the stock price to move.

Day Trading, however, is tricky for two main reasons. Firstly, day traders often compete with professionals, and secondly, they tend to have psychological biases that complicate the trading process.

Professional day traders understand the traps and tricks of this form of trading. In addition, they leverage personal connections, trading data subscriptions, and state-of-the-art technology to succeed. However, they still make losing trades. Some of these professionals are high-frequency traders whose aim is to skim pennies off every trade.

The Day Trading field is a crowded playground, which is why professional day traders love the participation of inexperienced traders. Essentially, it helps them make more money. In addition, retail traders tend to hold on to losing trades too long and sell winning trades too early.

Due to the urge to close a profitable trade to make some money, retail investors sort of pick the flowers and water the weeds. In other words, they have a strong aversion to making even a small loss. This tends to tie their hands behind their backs when it comes to purchasing a declining asset. This is due to the fear that it might decline further.

How to Start

People who want to start Day Trading should do several things to put themselves on the right path. Firstly, they need to step back and ask themselves whether this form of trading is really for them. Day Trading is not for the faint of heart. It requires a high level of focus and is not something people should risk their retirement plan to do.

Actually, beginners should consider opening a practice account before committing their hard-earned money. Reputable brokerage firms provide such accounts or stock market simulators to aspiring traders, through which they can make hypothetical trades and see the results.

In addition, aspiring day traders need to have a suitable brokerage account before they begin trading. Some brokers charge high transaction costs, which can erode the gains from winning trades. In addition, good brokers provide research resources that are invaluable to traders.

Aspiring traders who discover that Day Trading is not for them should do what smart investors do, which is engaging in long-term investing in a diversified fund or stock portfolio. They should regularly add more funds to their accounts and let the magic of growth expand their investment portfolio. This may not be as thrilling as Day Trading, but it is better than doing something that will clean out one's savings.

Consider Constraints and Goals

Before investing the time, energy, and effort in learning or creating and then practicing Day Trading, prospective day traders should consider their constraints and goals. For example:

1. Traders need to determine whether they have enough capital to engage in Day Trading. If they lack the capital, they should wait until they have it while they are learning about and practicing different trading strategies.

2. They should understand that achieving consistent gains takes several months to a year, even when practicing several hours each day. For those who practice intermittently, it will take longer to achieve

success; therefore, prospective traders should put in the time and effort required to achieve their goals.

3. Once they start trading, they need to commit to trading for at least two hours a day, depending on their commitments.

4. Until their trading profits match or surpass their income, new day traders should not quit their day jobs. They also need to determine the ideal time of day to trade based on their other commitments. In addition, they should ensure that their trading strategy fits that time of day. Essentially, their trading strategy needs to fit their life.

5. People who want to venture into Day Trading need to determine whether they want to do it with the aim of quitting their regular jobs. To get to the point where they can replace their day jobs by Day Trading, prospective traders need to understand that they will probably need to practice and trade for a year or more, depending on their dedication.

Aspiring day traders should consider the factors above before investing their time and money in learning this line of trade.

Choose a Broker

While new traders are practicing and developing their trading strategies, they should set aside some time to choose a good and reputable broker. It may be the same broker they opened a demo or practice account with, or it may be another broker. Actually, choosing the right broker is one of the most important transactions day traders will make because they will entrust the broker with all of their capital.

Capital Needed to Start Day Trading

How much capital people need to start Day Trading depends on the market they trade, where they trade, and the style of trading they wish to do. There is a legal minimum capital requirement set by the stock market to day trade; however, based on the individual trading style, there is also a recommended minimum.

A day trader needs to have enough capital to have the flexibility to make a variety of trades and withstand a losing streak, which will inevitably happen. Traders also need to determine the amount of money they need, which requires them to address risk management. In addition, they should not risk more than 2% of their account on a single trade.

Capital is the most important component when it comes to Day Trading. By risking only 1% or 2%, even a long losing streak will keep most of the capital intact. For day traders in the United States, the legal minimum balance needed to day trade stocks is $25,000. Traders whose balance drops below this amount cannot engage in Day Trading until they make a deposit that brings their balance above $25,000.

To have a buffer, U.S. day traders should have at least $30,000 in their trading accounts. Stocks usually move in $0.01 increments and trade in lots of 100 shares; therefore, with at least $30,000 in their accounts, day traders will have some flexibility.

Day traders can usually get leverage up to four times the amount of their capital. A trader with $30,000 in his/her account, for example, can trade up to $120,000 worth of stock at any given time. Essentially, the trade price multiplied by the position size can equal more than the trader's account balance. Day traders can trade fewer volatile stocks, which often require a bigger position size and a smaller stop loss, or stocks that are more volatile, with often require a smaller position size and a larger stop loss. Either way, the total risk on each trade should not be more than 2% of the trading account balance.

Day Trading Basics

Day Trading, on the surface, looks like it should be relatively easy. New day traders think it is all about making several simple trades as the price moves, making a little money, and repeating the whole process tomorrow. However, many dangers lurk in the Day Trading markets; unfortunately, a large percentage of new day traders are not aware of these dangers.

Some of the pitfalls for day traders include:

Lack of Risk Management

Often new day traders often lack risk management protocols, which is a huge danger. Sometimes, they have an incomplete strategy for managing risk. Nevertheless, they are usually optimistic about their Day Trading abilities, which often causes them to overlook critical risk management steps. Establishing a basic risk management strategy involves the following steps:

- **A Stop Loss**

    Traders should place a stop-loss order in each trade they make to control their risk. People who are starting out on Day Trading should limit their risk on each trade to 1% of their trading account balance. The difference between their entry price and stop-loss price, multiplied by their position size, is their risk.

- **A Daily Limit**

    A daily-stop loss limit can help day traders by limiting how much money they can lose in a day. If day traders suffer multiple losing trades each day, they may still find themselves down more than 10% in a single day.

A typical daily-stop loss limit should not be more than about 3% of a trader's account.

Therefore, if the trader loses 3% on any given day, he/she will stop trading for that day. As day traders develop a profitable trading record and gain experience, they can adjust their daily-stop loss limit to be equal to their average profitable trading day. By placing this limit, a typical winning day will recoup the losses from a single day.

Improperly Tested or Untested Trading Strategies

New day traders are often so eager to start trading and make money that they start using untested or improperly tested trading strategies with real money. Others, however, try out their strategies on demo accounts, and if they make a few successful trades, they immediately start trading with real money. Unfortunately, both of these approaches will probably lead to future disappointment.

Successful day traders, on the other hand, test their strategies on many different market conditions through demo trading to learn the pros and cons of their strategies before using them with real money. They demo trade for several months until they are comfortable with their Day Trading strategies before risking real capital with their strategies.

Broker

Choosing the right broker is one of the most important trades for a day trader. Day traders deposit their capital with their brokers, and yet some of them do not take the time to research their broker until a problem arises. Scam brokers, for example, can pop up anywhere.

Traders who find themselves working with such a broker will find it very difficult or even impossible to withdraw their money and any profits. Fortunately, scam brokers usually do not last long thanks to forum complaints. Therefore, a careful online search will reveal any problems with a broker.

A more subtle broker problem is constantly slow quotes. Day traders need direct and uninterrupted access to their broker, who then sends their orders to the appropriate exchange. They should test their broker's trading software because poor software will make it hard to execute trades in a timely manner.

Technology

No one is immune to technology problems. For example, computers can crash, power can go out, the internet can go down, and much more. Day traders cannot get out of a losing trade quickly if technology fails; therefore, they need to place a stop-loss order on every trade.

In addition, they need to program their broker's phone number into their cell phone and landline phone, so they can call them quickly in case of a problem. It is a good idea to have a mobile version of their trading platform on their internet-enabled mobile devices, which might still be operational if their computer crashes.

Order Types

The profits and losses day traders make come from the orders they place. Day traders should know their order types for getting in and out of a market order or a limit order. They also need to know how to set profit targets and stop-loss orders, both for going short and long.

For professional day traders, placing orders is automatic, like switching on a car's turn signal, when about to change lanes. Day traders who do not know their order types will have slow and clumsy trading or even place the wrong order type, which will cost them money.

It is normal for some trading mistakes to happen; however, compounding such mistakes with order-related trading mistakes is a recipe for disaster. Before they start trading, new day traders should know their order types.

Trader Personality and Tendencies

Another hidden danger for a new day trader is his/her personality and tendencies. In the beginning, Day Trading will be confusing, infuriating, and stressful in a way a new trader never thought it could. There are endless possibilities in the markets, and no one cares what anyone else is doing.

This freedom, however, can be unnerving and dangerous for many traders, which is why many of them lose money. When people are starting out, they do not know how they will react under different stresses and pressures. Some choose to quit, others to overtrade, and others still are too afraid to trade.

Many distractions keep people from staying focused and trading effectively. Traders should take a critical look at their personality to identify their shortcomings and then work to develop these six important Day Trading traits.

Volume, Price, Technical Indicators

Day traders can use technical indicators to provide trading signals and assess the current trade. Keltner Channels, a popular technical indicator, use average prices and volatility to plot lower, middle, and upper lines. These three lines move with the price to create the appearance of a channel.

Chester Keltner introduced these channels in the 1960s, but Linda Bradford Raschke updated them in the 1980s. Today, traders use the later version of the indicator, which is a combination of two different indicators, which are the average true range and the exponential moving average.

Created by J. Welles Wilder Jr. and introduced in 1978, the average true range is a measure of volatility. The moving average, on the other hand, is the average price for specific periods, with the exponential variation giving more weight to recent prices and less weight to less recent prices.

Keltner Channels are useful to day traders because they make trends more visible. When a certain asset or stock is trending higher, its price will frequently come close, touch, or even move past the upper band. In addition, the price will stay above the lower band and middle band, although it might occasionally barely dip below the middle band.

When an asset or stock is trending lower, on the other hand, its price will regularly come close to the lower band or reach it; however, sometimes it will move past the lower band. The price will stay below the upper band and often below the middle band.

Day traders should set up their indicators so that these guidelines hold true, at least most of the time. If the price of a stock is moving constantly higher but not reaching the upper band, the channel may be too wide, and the trader will need to decrease the multiplier. However, an asset that is trending higher but constantly touching the lower band shows that the channel is too tight, requiring an increase of the multiplier.

For their indicator to help them analyze the market, day traders need to adjust it correctly. If they fail to do this, then the guidelines for trading will not hold true, and the indicator will not serve its intended purpose.

Once they set up the indicator correctly, day traders should purchase during an uptrend when the price of the asset pulls back to the middle band.

They should place a target price somewhere near the upper band and a stop-loss order halfway between the lower and middle bands. On the other hand, if the price of the asset is hitting the stop-loss too often, and the trader has already made the necessary adjustments, he/she should move the stop-loss a bit closer to the lower band.

This will give the trade more wiggle room and reduce the number of losing trades the trader has. During a downtrend, when the price of the asset rallies to the middle band, day traders should short sell, which means selling the asset with the hope of buying it back at a lower price.

It is also important to place a target near the lower band and a stop-loss order about halfway between the upper and middle bands. This trading strategy leverages the trending tendency and provides trades with a 0.5 risk to reward ratio. This is because the stop-loss point is approximately half the length of that of the target price.

However, traders should not trade all pullbacks to the middle line. If a trend is not present, this strategy will not work effectively. Sometimes, the price of the asset moves back and forth between hitting the lower and upper bands. This method will not be effective in such situations.

Therefore, day traders should ensure the market's pattern is following the trending guidelines. If it is not doing so, they should use a different strategy. The Keltner Channel strategy tries to capture big moves that may evade the trend-pullback strategy. Day traders should use it near the opening of a major market when big movements happen.

The typical trading strategy is to purchase when the price breaks the upper band or sell short when it drops below the lower band within the first 30 minutes of the market opening. The middle band, however, acts as the exit point. This type of trade does not have a profit target. Traders simply exit the trade whenever the price touches the middle band, whether the trade is a winner or a loser.

> Introduction to Investing in Stocks, Options, and Forex

When most people hear the term Day Trading, they think of the stock market. However, day traders also participate in the forex and futures markets. Some day traders, for example, trade options, but most traders who do so are more likely swing traders who can hold positions for weeks or days, but not fractions of a trading day.

People who want to be successful day traders should initially focus on a single market, such as the stock market. Once they master that market, they can try to learn and practice trading other markets if they choose.

Day Trading Stocks

Those who are thinking of Day Trading stocks should consider a few important factors. These are:

1. Under U.S. law, the minimum starting capital for Day Trading stocks is $25,000. However, they need to add a buffer above this amount and start with a capital of at least $30,000.

2. Market hours for Day Trading are from 9:30 am to 4 pm Eastern time. However, traders can still place trades one hour before the market opens.

3. The ideal periods to day trade stocks are from 8.30 to 10.30 am and 3 to 4 pm ET, when volatility and volume are high.

4. Day traders can trade a wide variety of stocks. They can also trade the same stock or a small number of stocks every day, or find new stocks to trade each week or even each day.

Based on these factors, prospective day traders will determine whether the stock market is a good option for their Day Trading. If they do not have the initial capital required, for example, they should consider the futures or forex markets, which require less starting capital.

In addition, if they cannot trade during the most ideal trading hours, their efforts will not produce as much fruit as they would have if they were available during those optimal hours.

Day Trading Futures

Some of the important things to consider about Day Trading futures include

1. There is no legal minimum starting capital required to begin Day Trading futures. Experts, however, recommend starting with $2,500 to $7,000 if one is trading the popular futures contract. The more money one starts with, the more flexible one will be when it comes to making trading decisions.

2. The official market hours for trading the S&P 500 and E-mini are from 9.30 am to 4 pm ET.

3. The optimal time to day trade ES futures is from 6.30 to 1030am and 3 to 4p Eastern time.

4. Commodities futures contracts also provide reliable Day Trading opportunities.

5. Most day traders who deal with futures often focus on one futures contract; however, others choose futures contracts seeing significant volume or movements on a particular day.

Day Trading Forex

Things to know about Day Trading forex include:
1. The minimum starting capital required is $500; however, experts recommend starting with $5,000 if one wants a decent monthly income stream.

2. Forex trades 24 hours a day; however, certain times are ideal for Day Trading than others.

3. Day traders can trade any different currency pairs, but beginners should stick to the GBP/USD or EUR/USD. These two currency pairs offer more than enough price movement and volume to generate a good income.

Based on these three factors, day traders will likely determine whether this market is appropriate for them to day trade. Those with limited capital should consider Day Trading the forex market, which is more flexible than other markets.

Social Trading

Social trading works somewhat like a social network. However, there is a big difference, which is that instead of sharing pet photos, dinner photos, and selfies, people use social trading networks to share trading ideas. Essentially, traders use this platform to interact, brainstorm and watch the trading results of other professionals in real-time.

Some of the benefits of social trading include:

1. Access to reliable and helpful trading information

2. Ability to earn while learning
3. Quick understanding of the trading market
4. Ability to build a trading community of investors

Since social trading networks cater for both professionals and beginners, they create a reliable trading community, which allows day traders and other types of market traders to generate an income as they learn.

The allure of this form of financial trading is undeniable. It is more exciting for a trader to earn a living working from the comfort of his/her home, rather than working a regular 9 am to 5 pm gig. However, inexperienced or careless day traders can destroy their portfolios within a few days.

Chapter 4   How to Reduce Your Risks When Day Trading

Like any kind of investment, day trading does come with some risks. And day trading is often considered an even riskier option compared to some of the other investments you can choose. As a beginner, these risks may seem overwhelming and you may worry that this is not the right investment vehicle for you. There are a few things that you can do to help limit your risks as much as possible, including the following.

Only Trade What You Can Afford to Lose

When you enter a trade, make sure that you only trade the amount of money that you are comfortable with losing. There is a chance, especially when you are a beginner, when you may pick a bad trade and can lose money in the process. If you bet too much money on this, if you used leverage, or you made false assumptions about how the market would go, you could end up in big financial straights in the end.

Before you enter into day trading, consider setting aside a savings account. Take some time to put some money in savings before you get started, and add to it as you make profits. Only use the money in this account when you are trading. That way, when it is gone, you stop. And you didn't put your regular income or regular savings in jeopardy in the process.

Set up Your Stop Loss Points

Before you go into a trade, it is important to set up your entry and exit points. These are going to help maximize your profits like minimizing the potential losses that you could have. You need to have an idea of what price point the stock needs to be at for you to enter the trade. And then you need to have stop points for both ends of the spectrum for your profits and your losses.

Setting a stop point for losses can ensure that you only lose so much money. There are times when the market will plummet very quickly. If you don't have this in place, the market could slip down and you could lose a ton of money in a short amount of time. This stop point tells the brokerage account when you want to leave the market so you can limit your losses as much as possible.

You also want an exit strategy when it comes to how much money you want to make as profits. While this may seem silly as a trader, you want to earn as much as possible.

But since there is a lot of variability in the market during the day, the market can often reach a high point and turn, without going back up again. Setting this point helps you to earn as much profit as possible without you staying in the market too long.

Work with a Broker

As a beginner, it is often best to work with a broker if you can. This can open up a lot of different resources to you that can make day trading more profitable. The right broker can be someone you bounce ideas off, someone you can ask questions to, and someone who can give you advice on the best stocks to follow for your trading.

You can also pick your broker based on the fees that they charge. Each broker is going to be a little different. Some charge a flat rate based on how many trades that you want to do. If you plan to do a lot of trades here, which is common for day trading, you may not want to go with that option. If you are spending $4 for every trade you do, this is going to add up quickly when you do a bunch of trades through that broker.

Another option is to work on commission with the broker. This way, you only pay a percentage of the profits that you earn on the trades you do. This can be helpful as long as you make sure that you earn enough on the trades that you can cover the commissions and fees, and still have some money left over for profits in your pockets.

Stick with the Strategy You Chose Through the Whole Trade

After you take a look through some of the strategies we will discuss in this guidebook, you should have an idea of which one will work the best for you. Make sure to pick one that makes sense for you, has the number of risks that you are willing to take, and that works with your trading profile.

Once you pick a trading strategy, you need to stick with it, at least during that trade. Many beginner traders end up failing and losing a lot of money because they enter a trade using one strategy and then they move into a second strategy at some point during the same trade. Sometimes this is because they see they will lose money and they want to make changes to prevent this. Other times, they do it simply because they didn't fully understand the strategy they chose. Either way, it can result in disaster for that trade.

If you start with a trading strategy and find that it is not the right one for you, then finish of the trade and try a new strategy on the next trade. You may lose some money on that first trade, but you will limit the loss quite a bit compared to switching strategies right in the middle.

Take a Break from Trading When You Need It

Sometimes, you are going to run into a trade that is bad. You may not have put in the right exit points, or you may have picked the wrong strategy and it didn't work out well for you. This can be hard especially if you are a new trader and it is one of your first trades. After this bad trade happens, or if you seem to be making bad trade after bad trade, it is time to take a break. At this point, if you stay in the market, you will let your emotions take over and you will continue to make bad trading decisions. You may want to make a lot of income from day trading but sticking in the market when your emotions are involved, and after having a bad time with trading, it's just going to make things worse.

The break doesn't have to be a long time. Even a few days to a week can be enough to help you refocus and come back with a fresh look on your trading. It can be hard to take a break. You want to try a new idea, you want to make the money you lost back, and you don't want to give up. But taking a break doesn't mean you have given up. It simply means that you are giving yourself time to think critically the next time you trade.

Learn How to Keep the Emotions out of the Game

With any type of trading, if you let your emotions get into the game, then you have lost. This can be hard for many people especially if they put more money than they can afford to lose into a trade. With day trading, emotions can be an even bigger issue because the market changes so rapidly and you have to get in and out as quickly as possible.

When you allow your emotions to start coming into play, you are basically losing all of your control to make smart decisions. No one can make good decisions when the emotions are involved, and with all the stress and issues that can come with day trading, those emotions will hit some extremes pretty quickly. This is why it is so important to go through and pick out a winning strategy and to stick with it. This will keep the emotions at bay and you can make the decisions ahead of time before the emotions of being in the market come into play.

If you are in a trade and find that your emotions are starting to get in your way, it is time to make some changes. In some cases, you will be able to stick with your stop points and be safe for the rest of the trade. But if you have already gone through and left the stop points behind, it is time to leave the trade, no matter where it is going, and restart. You may even need to take a little time off from day trading, especially after a trade that did not do that well, so that you can regroup and get back to the critical thinking.

Don't Follow the Trends

If you are jumping onto a stock that everyone else is as well, then you are already getting to the party too late. As soon as others start purchasing or selling a stock, the price has already changed and you are too late. This could result in you paying too much for a stock, or selling it for too little because you got caught up in the trend.

As a day trader, it is your job to learn to spot trends before they happen. If you read the news, look through the right charts, and use your knowledge about the market, you can easily jump onto a stock before the trend happens. When you do this successfully, you would then purchase the stock while the price is lower, before others catch on. Then, when others catch onto the value of that stock, the price will go up where you can sell it for a higher price than you originally purchased it.

You can use this idea when selling the stock as well. If you know that a stock has a price ceiling of $55 and the stock is currently at $54.99, or even above $55, then it is time to sell. In the short trading period that you get with day trading, you won't really see the price of a stock go much above its ceiling price ever. You can see this trend and sell the stock at that high point before the market drags it back down and you lose money.

Day traders do not jump onto a trend because they know it means that they are too late for the party on that particular security. They learn how to read the trends through their own research and can accurately predict the best times to purchase and sell the stock to make the most profit.

Chapter 5   Finding and Picking Stocks and Trading Strategies

In this chapter, we get down to the actual work of day trading. We will cover how to read the market by discussing the types of charts used by day traders and how to read them. We'll also discuss strategies for picking stocks and what to look for in stocks for day trading. Finally, we'll cover the most common trading strategies and how to execute them.

Reading the Market

We've already discussed charts and charting software in passing. Now you need to know how to read the charts your software or your broker provide to you. There's three basic types of charts you're likely to look at when you're reading the market: line charts, bar charts, and "candlestick" charts.

Line Charts: line charts are the simplest type of chart you are likely to use while day trading. A line chart tracks only the closing prices for your selected time interval and will display as a jagged line from left to right. This is the type of chart you are probably most familiar with outside of the world of trading, and it provides the least information of the common chart types. However, many traders still use line charts for certain trading strategies. Since a line chart is less cluttered, it can make inflection points in the market more obvious to the eye and can be useful for drawing lines to identify ranges or trends.

Bar Charts: bar charts, also known as OHLC bar charts or HLC bar charts, include information on the open (O), high (H), low (L), and close (C) price of an asset over a given time interval. The chart will appear as a series of horizontal lines following the same sort of jagged line you would see in a simple line chart, with a small line jutting from each side at the open and close. There's a lot of information in these charts, so it may take quite a bit of practice to get used to reading them.

Open: the open on a bar chart is the opening price for the time interval and shows on the chart as a small line sticking out of the left side of the bar.

High: the high price during the interval is indicated by the top of the bar.

Low: the low price for the interval is indicated by the bottom the bar.

Close: the closing price for the interval shows as a small line sticking out of the right side of the bar.

Direction: you can tell the direction of the market during the interval by comparing the positions of the opening and closing prices for the interval. If the open is higher, the market is moving down. If the close is higher, the market is moving up.

Candlestick Charts: candlestick charts contain the same information as bar charts but presented in a different fashion that many traders find easier to read. At a glance, the candlestick chart will look similar to a bar chart, but more colorful. Each time interval will display as a colored bar (the "body" of the candle), red or green, with a line (the "tail") extending some distance above and below the body of the candlestick. Here's how the information is represented:

High: the high price for the interval is indicated by the top of the tail above the candle.

Low: the low price for the interval is indicated by the bottom of the tail below the candle.

Open: the opening price for the interval is indicated by the bottom of the body of the candle.

Close: the closing price for the interval is indicated by the top of the body of the candle.

Direction: the direction of the market is indicated by the color of the body of the candle - red if the market is moving down, green if the market is moving up.

Chart Parameters: when generating a chart, you will need to pick the interval that will be represented by each point in your chart. The interval could be based on time, "tick", volume, or price range.

A chart generated by time is the most intuitive, and will generate a new bar, candle, or point based purely on the passage of time - even if very few or even no transactions occurred during the interval. This is the most useful way to generate a chart if you are looking to see how a stock or asset performs in real time.

A chart generated by "tick" uses an interval based on a set number of transactions. For example, if you generate a 200-tick chart, the graph will produce a new point every time 200 transactions occur. This can be useful for comparing trends between stocks with different levels of activity.

A chart generated by volume will generate intervals based on a set number of shares exchanged.

You will also need to define the scope of the chart. Depending on your strategy, you may want to look at a chart for the entire trading day, or a chart that covers the last minute.

Trend lines: most trading software allows you to draw your own trend lines on charts or will have options for displaying trends such as the simple moving average automatically.

While you can get a lot of information just from your chart without trends, most of the decisions you will make in executing your trading strategy will come from looking at trend lines.

Picking Stocks

Now that you know the basics of reading the market and looking for trends, you're ready to learn about how to pick stocks for day trading. The type of stock you will be looking for depends on a lot of different factors, and you may be looking for different types of stocks to fit different trading plans and different trading strategies. We'll cover this topic in three parts: (1) things you should look for every stock you plan to trade while day trading; (2) some broad-based picking strategies for different trading plans; and (3) the distinct characteristics of stocks that are suitable for specific day-trading strategies.

(1) Things to Look for in Every Stock You Plan to Day-Trade: while what you're looking for will be different depending on what strategy you're planning to execute, there are a couple things you should always be looking for when picking stocks.

The first is volume: you should always look for stocks that have a high level of daily activity. If you buy into a stock with insufficient volume, you can easily find yourself stuck - the asset price won't move enough for you to take profit and you'll lose out on other trading opportunities until you can move out of your position.

Typically, you should be looking for a stock that has an average daily volume of at least 1 million shares.

The second is volatility: you are looking for stocks that will move enough in a typical day for you to make a profitable trade. Set your stock filter to look for stocks with an average day range above 5% over the last 50 days. It's important to remember that volatility is not necessarily the massive up or down swings that can follow breaking news - it can also be the regular and constant turbulence that exists in all exchange traded markets.

(2) Broad Strategies for Picking Stocks: you need a broad strategy for picking stocks beyond simply looking for the desirable characteristics discussed in this chapter. How you go about researching and picking stocks depends on how much time you have available to trade and how much research you are willing to do.

If you don't have much time to trade, you may wish to specialize. That is, pick one or two stocks, or a single industry sector (such as healthcare), and only trade in those stocks or that sector. This lets you become an expert in those stocks: you know how they usually behave, where the opportunities will be, and what news events will cause swings and how. This means that you don't have to spend a lot of time sifting through charts or learning the basic facts about new companies - you already know what's likely to happen. A popular way to execute this strategy is to target an ETF, such as the S&P 500 SPDR (Ticker symbol SPY). Specializing like this works well with a range-trading or "trade the news" strategy.

If you're looking for a little bit more flexibility, you might choose to pick a set of stocks to trade each week. Each weekend, run a stock screener to identify a set of 2-4 stocks that have good volume and volatility for your trading strategy. After you have picked your stocks for the week, trade those stocks, and only those stocks following your trading plan. If you've achieved good results, you could choose to remain on the same set of securities for multiple weeks in a row. This strategy is suitable for a trader who has a little more time to dedicate to day trading but isn't prepared to trade full time.

If you're looking to pursue a full-time career as a day trader, you might choose to run a stock screener every single day. This is probably what you want to be doing if you are pursuing a momentum strategy - as you will be trying to identify stocks that have a strong current trend, instead of trying to capitalize on small movements caused by underlying volatility. Obviously, this strategy is very time consuming, and may require additional tools to execute effectively.

(3) Distinct Characteristics Suitable for Specific Strategies: depending on your strategy, you may be looking for more specific factors than simple volume and volatility.

If you are looking to trade on a momentum strategy, you should look at stocks that are close to 52-week highs and lows. Stocks that have reached extreme price points are more likely to be volatile or to be close to an inflection point that can afford a big trading opportunity.

You may also want to keep an eye out for stocks that have a gap against the trend. That is, if you look at your chart of the stock's current price, you'll see that there is a space (a "gap") between the price and the trend-line. This is a good way to identify stocks that have been overbought or oversold, or where the stock price has failed to adjust to breaking news. The moment when the gap closes is the moment when you have an opportunity to make a profitable trade.

Finally, you can set up a scanner to identify specific situations where there is an opportunity to trade based on a specific pattern in the market. One example of this is a method commonly referred to as "sniper" trading, which was originally implemented on the FOREX market.

An Overview of Common Day Trading Strategies

By sticking to your strategy, you maintain a stable level of risk and can reliably make your expected earnings goals. Here's a quick overview of some of the most common strategies for setting entry points and price targets.

Scalping: **Scalping is one of the most common strategies for day trading, and with good reason - it's incredibly simple. When you are using a scalping strategy, your target price is essentially whatever price is high enough to make your trade profitable over commission. It's as easy as that: pick your asset, pick your entry point, and sell as soon as it's profitable for you. As always, make sure you have set a stop-loss if you have misjudged the buy and bought into a downward trend.**

Fading: In many ways, a fading strategy is the opposite of scalping. When you are scalping, you are looking to profit on an upward trend - while fading, you are looking to profit on a downward trend. Scalping is absurdly simple, while fading requires a fairly high degree of sophistication to be really successful. Here's a basic overview: a trader who is using a fade strategy looks for a stock that has risen very quickly. Having identified a potential trade, the trader shorts the stock. The price target is a predicted low inflection point where buyers begin to step in after profit-takers exit.

This probably seems counter intuitive to a trader starting out, since it requires you to bet a stock that has been on an upward tear is going to fall in the same day. So, here's a quick explanation of the reasoning behind a fade strategy: (1) a stock that has risen very quickly is probably overbought - the price has been driven higher than demand can justify; (2) early buyers are probably ready to start profit taking - you can expect that traders who bought into the trend early are ready to unload stock, dropping the price; and (3) existing buyers may be scared out of purchasing at the current, inflated price - creating an opportunity to short the stock at a point below the peak, but above where the upward trend started.

Fading is a risky strategy, since it requires you to identify a very specific situation - but, as always, higher risk can yield higher rewards than a low-risk strategy like scalping. You may wish to consider a fading strategy after you have gotten comfortable reading the market if you can afford the additional risk.

Momentum Trading: generally speaking, momentum trading is a simple sounding strategy that can get complicated fast. When you are using a momentum strategy, you are looking to identify an existing market trend that you expect to continue for some time. While trading using a momentum strategy, use your tools to look for a consistent upward or downward trend - but not, for example, the sort of extreme upward trend you would be looking for under a pure fading strategy.

If you have identified an upward trend, under a momentum strategy, you buy in while the stock is rising, much like under a scalping strategy. Unlike scalping, however, you aren't looking to sell at the minimum point where you can make a profit. Instead, you're aiming to set your price target at the inflection point where the price will begin to fall. This can be done either by monitoring the current prices and charts and selling as soon as you observe momentum shifting, or by setting a price target at a point where you are making a reasonable profit.

If you have identified a downward trend, you can also short under a momentum strategy. Like a normal fade strategy, you are looking to set your price target at a low inflection point where seller volume will decrease, and buyers will begin to re-enter the asset.

Trading the News: trading the news is a specific form of momentum trading that tries to identify an upward or downward trend before it even begins. If you are looking to execute on this strategy, you will be monitoring news headlines for events that will have an effect on a specific stock, a specific business sector, or even the market as a whole. Your goal is to correctly identify a market trend at the point it begins based on that news. This can allow you to increase your profit margin compared to a normal momentum strategy where you are simply buying into an existing trend.

There are regularly occurring, scheduled events that can be helpful to watch out for when trying to execute a news-based strategy. One example would be a publicly traded corporation's quarterly earnings calls. By listening in on an investor earning call, you can try to ascertain whether a company has done better or worse than it was expected to by market analysts. Depending on earnings performance, this can help you identify an upward or downward trend and set your positions early. Another example would be Federal Reserve meetings - the chairman's comments on the market or interest rates can put the entire market into an upward or downward trend on a dime.

Of course, everyone who is trading - especially the large, institutional investors - keeps an eye on scheduled events like this. This means it's hard to get a jump on the news - and big investors will get trades to go through faster than yours ever can. The real opportunities for profit come from unexpected events, or events whose market consequences aren't immediately obvious. If you think you're smarter than the market, maybe you can identify a rise or fall before it happens by taking in all the news you can find. However, betting on uncertain news or nascent trends is risky, and keep that in mind before you take action on an unusual news item.

Range Trading / Daily Pivots: **All of the strategies we've discussed so far are somewhat dependent on market conditions where you can discern clear up or down trends in a given asset. However, you can still make money in a very stable market with the strategy of range trading, by taking advantage of the natural, low level volatility that exists in the market - the "noise" or "turbulence" that is always present. Here's a three-step summary of how to execute a range-based strategy:**

(1) Identify the daily range of an asset. Your goal in a range strategy is to identify the daily high and low points of the target asset that are caused by natural market volatility, identifying the points of support and resistance that cause price inflection. The easiest way to do this is to pull up a longer-term chart, such as the 4-hour simple moving average, and draw a horizontal line across matching peaks and troughs. The peaks should exist at the point of resistance, where the asset is overbought and demand cannot sustain a higher price. The troughs should exist at points of support - where the asset is under bought and the supply is insufficient to meet demand at a lower price.

(2) Time your entry so you are buying into the asset when it is priced in the support zone. This is what you expect to be the market low for the day.

(3) Manage your risk. Even though this strategy is looking to take advantage of the predictable volatility in a stable market, you still need to appropriately manage your risk by setting a stop-loss in case you have misjudged the low and set your price target at the expected zone of resistance.

Chapter 6   Day Trading Tools

For you to carry out day trading successfully there are several tools that you need. Some of these tools are freely available, while others must be purchased. Modern trading is not like the traditional version. This means that you need to get online to access day trading opportunities.

Therefore, the number one tool you need is a laptop or computer with an internet connection. The computer you use must have enough memory for it to process your requests fast enough. If your computer keeps crashing or stalling all the time, you will miss out on some lucrative opportunities. There are trading platforms that need a lot of memory to work, and you must always put this into consideration.

Your internet connection must also be fast enough. This will ensure that your trading platform loads in real-time. Ensure that you get an internet speed that processes data instantaneously to avoid experiencing any data lag. Due to some outages that occur with most internet providers, you may also need to invest in a backup internet device such as a smartphone hotspot or modem. Other essential tools and services that you need include:

Brokerage

To succeed in day trading, you need the services of a brokerage firm. The work of the firm is to conduct your trades. Some brokers are experienced in day trading than others. You must ensure that you get the right day trading broker who can help you make more profit from your transactions. Since day trading entails several trades per day, you need a broker that offers lower commission rates. You also need one that provides the best software for your transactions. If you prefer using specific trading software for your deals, then look for a broker that allows you to use this software.

Real-time Market Information

Market news and data are essential when it comes to day trading. They provide you with the latest updates on current and anticipated price changes on the market. This information allows you to customize your strategies accordingly. Professional day traders always spend a lot of money seeking this kind of information on news platforms, in online forums or through any other reliable channels.

Financial data is often generated from price movements of specific stocks and commodities. Most brokers have this information. However, you will need to specify the kind of data you need for your trades. The type of data to get depends on the type of stocks you wish to trade.

Monitors

Most computers have a capability that enables them to connect to more than one monitor. Due to the nature of the day trading business, you need to track market trends, study indicators, follow financial news items, and monitor price performance at the same time. For this to be possible, you need to have more than one processor so that the above tasks can run concurrently.

Classes

Although you can engage in day trading without attending any school, you must get trained on some of the strategies you need to succeed in the business. For instance, you may decide to enroll for an online course to acquire the necessary knowledge in the business. You may have all the essential tools in your possession, but if you do not have the right experience, all your efforts may go to waste.

Day Trading Pricing Charts

Charts are used by traders to monitor price changes. These changes determine when to enter or exit a trading position. There are several charts used in day trading. Although these charts differ in terms of functionality and layout, they typically offer the same information to day traders.

Some of the most common day trading charts includes:

1. Line charts
2. Bar charts
3. *Candlestick charts*

For each of the above charts, you must understand how they work as well as the advantages/disadvantages involved.

Line Charts

These are very popular in all kinds of stock trading. They do not give the opening price, just the closing price. You are expected to specify the trading period for the chart to display the closing price for that period. The chart creates a line that connects closing prices for different periods using a line.

Most day traders use this chart to establish how the price of a security has performed over different periods. However, you cannot rely on this chart as the only information provider when it comes to making some critical trading decisions. This is because the chart only gives you the closing price. This means that you may not be able to establish other vital factors that have contributed to the current changes in the price.

Bar Charts

These are lines used to indicate price ranges for a particular stock over time. Bar charts comprise vertical and horizontal lines. The horizontal lines often represent the opening and closing costs. When the closing price is higher than the opening price, the horizontal line is always black. When the opening price is higher, the line becomes red.

Bar charts offer more information than line charts. They indicate opening prices, highest and lowest prices as well as the closing prices. They are always easy to read and interpret. Each bar represents rice information. The vertical lines indicate the highest and lowest prices attained by a particular stock. The opening price of a stock is always shown using a small horizontal line on the left of each vertical line. The closing price is a small horizontal line on the right.

Interpreting bar charts is not as easy as interpreting line charts. When the vertical lines are long, it shows that there is a significant difference between the highest price attained by a security and the lowest price. Large vertical lines, therefore, indicate that the commodity is highly volatile while small lines indicate slight price changes. When the closing price is far much higher than the opening price, it means that the buyers were more during the stated period. This indicates likelihood for more purchases in the future. If the closing price is slightly higher than the purchase price, then very little purchasing took place during the period. Bar chart information is always differentiated using color codes. You must, therefore, understand what each color means as this will help you to know whether the price is going up or down.

Advantages of bar charts

- They display a lot of data in a visual format
- They summarize large amounts of data
- They help you to estimate important price information in advance
- They indicate each data category as a different color
- Exhibit high accuracy
- Easy to understand

Disadvantages

- They need adequate interpretation
- Wrong interpretation can lead to false information
- Do not explain changes in the price patterns

Tick charts

Tick charts are not common in day trading. However, some traders use these charts for various purposes. Each bar on the chart represents numerous transactions. For instance, a 415 chart generates a bar for a group of 415 trade positions. One great advantage of tick charts is that they enable traders to enter and exit multiple positions quickly. This is what makes the charts ideal for day traders who transact volumes of stock each day.

These charts work by completing several trades before displaying a new bar. Unlike other charts, these charts work depending on the activity of each transaction, not on time. You can use them if you need to make faster decisions in your trade. Another advantage of tick chart is that you can customize each chart to suit your trading needs. You can apply the chart on diverse transaction sizes. The larger the size, the higher the potential of making a profit from the trade.

When used in day trading, tick hart works alongside the following three indicators:

- *RSI indicators* – these are used when trading highly volatile securities. They help you establish when a particular security is oversold or overbought since these are the periods when stock prices change significantly.

- *Momentum* – day traders use this together with tick charts to show how active the stock price is and whether the activity is genuine or fake. If the price rises significantly, yet the momentum is the same, this indicates a warning sign. Stocks with positive momentum are ideal for long trades. You should avoid these if you wish to close your positions within a day.

- *Volume indicators* – these are used to confirm the correct entry and exit points for each trade. Large trading positions are often indicated using larger volume bars while low positions with little volatility are displayed using small volume bars.

Candlestick Charts

Candlestick charts are used on almost every trading platform. These charts carry a lot of information about the stock market and stock prices. They help you to get information about the opening, closing, highest, and lowest stock prices on the market. The opening price is always indicated as the first bar on the left of the chart, and the closing price is on the far right of the chart. Besides these prices, the candlestick chart also contains the body and wick. These are the features that differentiate the candlestick for other day trading charts.

One great advantage of candlestick charts entails the use of different visual aspects when indicating the closing, opening, highest, and lowest stock prices. These charts compute stock prices across different time frames. Each chart consists of three segments:

- The upper shadow
- The body
- The lower shadow

The body of the chart is often red or green in color. Each candlestick is an illustration of time. The data in the candlestick represents the number of trades completed within the specified time. For instance, a 10-minute candlestick indicates 10 minutes of trading. Each candlestick has four points, and each point represents a price. The high point represents the highest stock price while low stands for the lowest price of a stock. When the closing price is lower than the opening price, the body of the candlestick will be red in color. When the closing price is higher, the body will be colored green.

There are several types of candlesticks that you can use in day trading. One is the Heikin-Ashi chart that helps you to filter any unwanted information from the chart data, ending up with a more accurate indication of the market trend. Novice day traders commonly use this chart because of how clear it displays information.

The Renko chart only displays the changes in time. It does not give you any volume or time information. When the price exceeds the highest or lowest points reached before, the chart displays it as a new brick. The brick is white when the price is going up and black when the price is declining.

Lastly, the Kagi chart is used when you want to follow the direction of the market quickly. When the price goes higher than previous prices, the chart displays a thick line. When the price starts to decline, the line reduces in thickness.

Each of the above charts works using a time frame which is represented using the X-axis. This time frame always indicates the volume of information represented by the chart. Time frames can be in the form of standard time or in the form of the number of trades completed within a specified period as well as the price range.

Charting Software

Each of the above charts is created and viewed using specific software. This can be found in a brokerage firm, although you may also purchase this online depending on the type you want to use.

The software helps you identify the right opportunities by indicating when and how you should start and close positions. They always display the necessary patterns required to estimate future changes in stock prices. Using stock patterns, you can also establish continuations as well as reversals in the stock prices.

Chart software is available in many forms. You may find those that are in the form of mobile apps or others that are web-based. Getting the right software enables you to generate correct charts. This explains why you also need to incorporate technical analysis in your trades.

Most day trading chart tools are available free of charge. Some have a forum where you can learn from experienced traders as you use them. They also come with demo accounts that enable you to master day trading techniques before investing your capital in the business.

How to Choose Day Trading Charts

Before selecting any charts for your day trading engagements, you must consider a number of factors. These include:

1. *Responsiveness* - This refers to how quickly the chart can display information about the changing market features. This is the first and most important factor you should always check out for. Any delay in the way a chart displays data means that you will not receive vital information in real-time. You may end up acting on old information to make your

decisions, and this can lead to significant losses on your part. Most charts may freeze or crash when your computer runs out of memory. This explains why you need a fast processing machine for your day trading business. You want to ensure that the whole process remains as efficient as possible. When testing a chart for responsiveness, wait for a time when the stock market is busy. For instance, you may try using the chart during a critical financial announcement or news session. If the chart freezes at this point, then you will understand that it is not the best for your needs.

2. *Cost* – every trader wants to invest in tools that cost less to acquire and maintain. Years back, trading charts used to cost a fortune. This limited the number of traders that could engage in day trading. For instance, traders could buy market data from stock exchanges, and this would also cost a lot of money. Nowadays, all information required for any kind of trading is cheaply available.

This means that charts should also not cost as much. There are several alternatives available on the market today for you to select from. As you do this, always have the price in mind.

3. *Stability* – a good chart is one that remains online and up to date all the time. For you to succeed as a day trader, you must remain on the market most of the time. If your chart keeps disconnecting from the stock market or fails to display market information on time, then it will make you incur more losses. You must, therefore, ensure that you remain connected to the market continuously. If you experience instability as a result of the chart software you are using, feel free to change it. If the instability is resulting from a poor internet connection, you may need to replace it too.

4. *Type of Indicators* – if you have ever engaged in day trading before then you understand the importance of technical indicators. Having the right indicators plays a vital role in ensuring you predict the right

price movements in the future. Indicators help you to save a lot of capital. They prevent you from making important investment and financial mistakes that may lead to losing your capital. You may create your own indicators, or you may get charting software that has in-built indicators. If you decide to use your own indicators, you must ensure that the charting tools you purchase can be used together with these indicators. If not, you might need to stick to those indicators supplied together with your charting software.

5. *Compatibility with your computer* – before settling for any charts, check whether it will work well with your current computer resources. This is an important factor as it will determine whether you will continue to use your old machine, or if you will have to purchase a new one. Some charts require a lot of RAM space. If your computer does not have this capability, you will end up adding more RAM. This translates to more yet unnecessary costs. When you are looking

around for a chart, ensure that you check how much resources the charts will need. Most chart packages have an indication of the minimum requirements you need for the charts to work well. If this is not clearly stated, make sure you ask your provider about it so that you do not make a blind purchase.

6. *User-friendly* - a good chart should be easy to use, read, and interpret. A complicated chart will only make your trading days difficult. Get a chart that simplifies the work of interpreting data. Take your time and research on the available options then choose the best in terms of simplicity and layout. You may consider getting recommendations from other traders, although this does not necessarily mean that the said chart will work for you. Having a complicated chart can make you lose your confidence. You must, therefore, avoid it if you want to have a smooth trading experience

7. *End-user support* – once in a while, your chart software may experience a problem that needs technical assistance. As you continue using the software, questions may arise that need the attention of an expert. If the provider is not available to assist or respond to your questions, you may get stuck using the package. Before making a purchase, ensure that you find out the kind of technical support you will receive and how this will be done. Is it via live chat, email, or telephone contact? You can also go through some customer reviews just to understand if the service provider has a history of supporting its clients on technical matters. In case you need a highly responsive system, you may need to avoid those platforms that use the support ticket criteria. Companies that use this criterion to solve customer problems always take a long time to respond to even the most critical issues.

Charts play an essential role, and you can use timed as well as ticked charts for successful day trading. Always remember that different tools are designed for different kinds of trades. You must understand the kind of tools you need as a day trader so that you do not struggle on the market.

Chapter 7   Understanding Trading Orders

As a trader, you will need a broker through whom you will place buy or sell orders for any asset. You can decide whether you are going to buy or sell any stock, then place an order accordingly on your online trading platform.

Usually, Exchanges use a bid and ask process for fulfilling orders placed by traders. This means that there must be a buyer and seller to complete a single order, and they both should agree on the price. For example, if a trader wants to buy a stock at X price, there must be a seller willing to sell that stock at the same price. No transaction can occur unless a buyer and a seller agree at the same price.

The bid is the highest price a trader is willing to pay to buy an asset, and the ask is the lowest price, that trader is willing to accept to sell that asset. In stock markets, the price moment is directed by a tussle between the bid and ask prices. These prices keep constantly changing. As trading orders get filled, the price levels also keep changing, which is reflected in the technical charts.

While day trading, one must keep in mind this bid and ask process, because this will determine at what price the order will be executed. When markets are moving slowly, the change in price is also slow and one can wait to get the trading orders filled at the desired price. However; when markets are highly volatile and sees big up or down moves happen within split seconds, the order may get filled on a higher than expected rate. This can cause losses to day traders as the price changes quickly and can reverse by the time their orders are filled.

Different markets have different methods of matching buyers' and sellers' prices. These methods are called trading mechanisms. There are two main types of trading mechanisms; order-driven, and quote driven. In markets that use quote driven trading, a constant stream of prices (quotes) is available to traders. These prices are decided by market makers, therefore; these types of trading systems are better suited for over the counter (OTC) markets or dealers. There is a considerable spread between the bid and ask prices, which constitutes the profit of the deal maker or the market maker.

Exchanges mostly adopt the order-driven trading mechanism. Here, orders are executed when buy orders match with a sell order. In this type of trading mechanism, dealmakers are not involved.

Mechanism of Trading Orders

In the electronic day trading, orders are placed on the online trading platforms. These orders are the trader's instructions to the broker, or the brokerage firm, for buying or selling some security. When you are trading stocks, you place orders to buy or sell a stock, which is fulfilled by the brokerage firm with whom you have a trading account. The ease of electronic trading has given traders the freedom to initiate various types of order, where they can use different restrictions in order conditions. By these restrictions, traders can control the price and time of order execution. Such instructions help increase traders' profits or restrict the losses.

In systems, where the trading mechanism is order-driven, traders can also control the timeline of any specific order. For example, a trader can place an order which will remain open until its execution. Traders can also place orders that last till the end of the session, or one day, or a specific time.

Understanding how trading orders are placed, and how they can impact one's day trading, is important because it can affect once profit or loss in day trading. For example, a novice day trader may not be aware of the slippage between the bid and ask prices. There is always a difference between the bid and ask price is called slippage. It occurs in every trade, and every trader faces it whether buying, selling, entering a position or exiting from a position. This is also called the spread between a bid and ask price. So, when you place an order to buy a stock at $4, the slippage may increase its cost to $4.05 when your order is filled. Likewise; when you are existing any position, you place an order to sell at $3, but the slippage causes it to get filled at $2.98, thus chipping away at some of your profits.

Professional traders advise beginners to stay away from highly volatile market situations because the slippage risk increases during those choppy moments. For example; on a central bank policy declaration day, stock prices become highly volatile and move with big numbers within seconds. In such a situation, the ordered price and executed price may be different, causing financial harm to the day trader. From the outside, such big moves may look tempting to day traders and make them greedy, thinking they can make big profits with such huge price moves. But the reality is, the slippage between the bid and ask price is equally big and it can change considerably by the time the trading order gets filled, or immediately after the order is executed, creating a loss-making situation for the trader.

Different Types of Trading Orders

Most individual traders use a broker or dealers' trading platforms to place their trading orders. These platforms provide the facility of placing various types of orders, which are helpful in trade planning. Placing an order on the trading platforms is instructing the brokerage firm to buy or sell a financial asset on behalf of the trader. Based on the execution type, here are some common order types:

Market Orders: These orders do not have any specific price. A market order is an instruction to the broker to complete the trade at the available price. Because there is no fixed price, these orders almost always get executed, unless there is some liquidity problem. Traders use market orders when they want their trades executed quickly and they are not bothered about the execution price.

These orders are good if there is not much slippage between the bid and ask price. But a big slippage can cause loss to the traders, especially those who day trade in options.

Limit Orders: Traders place limit orders when they want to buy or sell stocks (or other assets) at a specific price. For example, if Apple shares are trading at $220, and traders expect the price to dip low, they can place a limit order to buy the shares at $219 or lower. Limit orders can be used for both buying and selling. Traders use these orders when they are trading with technical levels and are sure of price touching those level. For example, if a trader has bought Apple shares at $220, and thinks it can touch $222, he can place a limit order to sell his shares at that higher price. When the share price reaches that level, his sell order will get executed.

Stop Orders: These are also known as stop-loss orders and make a part of traders' money management techniques. A stop-loss order can stop the trade from going below a specific price, thus restricting losses for the trader. These orders are used for both buy and sell trades. The price specified in a stop-loss order is called stop price; and once that price is reached, the order is executed as a market order.

Day Order: This order Is valid only in the same trading session where it is placed. If the specified price is not achieved by the end of the session, the order is automatically canceled. This saves day traders from carrying forward their orders to the next day.

Preparations for Placing an Order

When preparing day trading plans and strategies, many day traders forget to pay attention that how they will place orders for trades. Believe it or not, the simple act of placing a trading order can have a big impact on the success of your day trading business.

Successful day traders always give importance to order processing techniques and plan their trades around the stock price they will focus during the trading. The trading plan itself means planning at what price you will enter a trade and when you will exit. Online trading platforms provide many methods of placing your orders around your planned trade prices. You can prepare charts of your trade, mark entry, and exit points and place orders for both trades together, or separately.

A good trading plan always includes trade entry, exit, profit booking, and loss stopping points. The margin trading facility provided by various brokerage firms also includes placing a stop-loss order together with the primary buy or sell order. This ensures that your trade will never suffer a loss beyond a specific price level. Here is an example to illustrate this:

Suppose a trader has bought stock 'A' at $10. He is expecting the price to go up, so he'll make some profit. However; anything can happen in stock markets and in case the price reverses, he wants to restrict his losses to $3 only. So, he will place a stop-loss order at $7, which is $3 below his buying price. If the price keeps moving up, the stop loss order will remain inactive. In case, the stock price falls, nothing will happen till it reaches $7, at which time the stop loss order will be triggered, and automatically sell the stock he has bought.

A stop-loss order makes sure that even if the trader is not available to check prices, his position will be safe till a certain price.

Similarly, traders can also use limit orders to exit their positions after earning a profit. Taking the above example once again, if a trader has bought a stock at $10, and believes that the price will move up to $15; he can place a limit order to sell at $15. When the price reaches his target ($15), it will be automatically executed, and the position will be squared off with a profit of $5.

These examples show that day traders can use a combination of different order types for money management and managing the risk and reward ratio. By technical analysis of any stock chart, day traders can find at what price the stock will make a big move, and be ready to place their orders near that price level.

Some other Order Types:

Apart from the basic orders, some other order types are not so common but can be used for money management or specific trading strategies.

For example, some day traders are more active during the market closing hours, as they create trading strategies for the next session. To take advantage of the price movement during the closing hours, they can place 'Limit-On-Close' (LOC) orders. As the name shows, it is a limit order and is specified for getting executed when markets close. As you know, a limit order controls at what price any security will be bought or sold. LOC has an extra parameter of 'on close', which adds another condition to this order, that it should only get executed if the closing price matches the order's price limit. For this order, both the limit price and the market's closing price are important.

Expert day traders use this order to take advantage of the closing time volatility in the stock markets, where they expect the price to reach a certain level. The LOC order has a drawback; if the closing price does not reach the limit price of the order, it is not executed. Also, this order must be placed within a specific time, before markets close for the day. The LOC order is valid only through the same trading session and is not carried forward to the next session.

Sometimes when the trader places this order but its requirements are not met for a while, the trader decides to wait till it gets executed. In that situation, it will be called an open order. The order will remain open until the trader does not actively cancel it. All open day orders get canceled automatically at the end of the session. During the session. If traders do not wish to wait further for the trade to take place, they will have to cancel all open orders manually. The open orders are often caused by buying or sell limit orders or stop orders. Traders can use GTC (good till canceled) option for their open orders, which will carry forward their orders until it is executed. Traders have the option to cancel the open order at any time.

When traders open any order and then decide not to get it executed, they can cancel it and it becomes a canceled order. This can happen when they mistakenly place a wrong order and upon realizing their mistake, immediately cancel the order. Or sometimes, they place a limit order, wait for it to get executed, then decide not to complete the trade and cancel the order. Market orders usually get immediately executed, so it is difficult to cancel a market order after it has been placed. But limit and stop orders have a time gap before getting executed. Therefore; traders can cancel these orders before their execution.

Overview

For stock trading, one needs to place buy or sell orders through a broker. There must be a buyer and seller to complete any order and they should agree on a specific price to complete the trade. Stock prices move through a process of the bid and ask. Day traders must keep this in mind when they are placing an order because the difference between the bid and ask price can cause slippage, which is harmful to a day traders' profits. Different markets have a different trading mechanism.

Online trading platforms facilitate order execution. Traders place their orders through the platform, which is executed by the brokerage firm. The time and method of order placing can impact one's day trading profits and losses. The spread or the difference between the bid and ask price can change at what price any trade is executed. Therefore; beginner day traders should stay away from volatile markets because, in those market conditions, the slippages can cause them considerable financial harm.

Day traders can use different order types to execute the trade. Market orders are executed almost immediately at the latest available price. These orders are good to use when markets are trending. Most of the time, day traders prefer to place limit orders where they can control the buy or sell price of their trades. Traders also used stop-orders to control the loss or to decide the profit booking levels in their trades. For intraday trading, traders can use the day order, which, if not fulfilled, gets canceled at the end of the session.

Order placing has an important place in traders' money management and trading strategies. Traders can pre-plan their trades and decide at what level they will buy or sell any stock. Technical analysis can help them find levels where the stock price will make considerable moments. They can place different orders near these price levels to manage their trades. Day traders can combine various orders to manage their risk and reward ratio.

Apart from the basic order types, there are many other orders, which expert traders use for their trading strategies. LOC or 'Limit-On-Close' Is one such order that traders can use to buy or sell stocks at the market-closing price. They can use this order type to take advantage of the closing hours' high volatility in markets, or if they are planning any strategy for the next day's opening session. Any order that is not filled is called an open order. Sometimes traders cancel their orders for various reasons, and these are called canceled orders.

Chapter 8   Money Management

What is Money Management?

Money management is not a new aspect of the financial management world. It started when there was a rise of capitalism. When the economy was under a system that was dominated by private owners, they had their private properties and gained on the profits. Money Management started in around 1600, and individuals only survive by depending on how effectively they get their income. In the present age, to be successful financially involves having the ability and the zeal to save more, and lean on investing any surplus.

Money management is a term to refer to the many ways people manage their financial resources. It ranges from budget planning in regards to their income. Money management involves planning and purchasing items that are important to you. Without planning well and lack of money management skills, the amount a person has will always not be enough for them.

Before anyone starts on the money management journey, you need to be aware of the assets and liabilities that you have. Some of the examples of Personal assets and properties are cars, home, retirement, investment, and bank accounts. On the other hand, personal liabilities are loans, debts, and mortgages. To be able to know your net worth, you should see the difference between your assets and liabilities. When the liabilities are higher than the assets, then you have a lower net worth. Having excellent money management skills, you will be able to avoid this.

Goal setting helps in Money management. Without goal setting, you will be worried about daily bill management; this can adversely affect your long term goals. With goal setting, you can have a clear view of the expenses needed to, and which needs to be cut out. A perfect example is when you have a goal of getting a car worth $30,000, your goals will be to cut down your expenses. Similar to someone whose goals are to get a $20,000 car?

After planning and knowing your goals, start creating your budget. A budget is an estimation of income for a defined period of time — a tool which will assist you in managing your money well. With a budget, you will be able to save some cash and be able to minimize impulse buying. An example of a reasonable budget will be to allocate $250 for entertainment and miscellaneous expenses a month after settling the basic needs. If your income increases, it would be advisable to add the extra income to your savings plan and not adding it to the expenses budget.

When budgeting, you will have multiple accounts to manage. For example, you may have an emergency fund and saving accounts. By doing this, you will avoid the temptations of spending the funds on impulse buying. The retirement plan should be kept separate from the other accounts. There are different software that you can use to assist you in money management. An example of a money management software is Quicken; it helps in tracking your various accounts and ensuring your saving and spending goals are on the right track.

The different aspects of money management include analyzing, planning, and executing a financial portfolio. The financial portfolio includes investment types, taxes, savings, and banking. In business management, there are economic variables that might affect your business finances. The best Money Management skills are to be able to access and control all the factors that might affect your financial position.

You can achieve your set goals through excellent money management. A dream of owning a home without using student loans, and be able to have a stress-free life from debts. Have a better plan to be able to deal with unpredictable events that can affect your finances; like loss of employment, serious illness. With Money Management, you will be able to have some savings that will cover your unexpected events.

Internet is a global computer network that contains information and provides communication. Banking, investment, and insurance needs did not exist before. In the past days, customers had restrictions on decisions making in their financial matters, with less information on their options in their local areas. With the lack of internet connection, there was limitation and restrictions on where to find the right information. People had to go shopping for different items, like furniture and electronics. And also the purchasing of mortgages and insurance policies.

Money Management Skills

Do you know your income expenditure? Do you know your shopping, clothing and entertainment expenses? Money Management is a life skill which is not in the school curriculum. Most people learn it from our parents on how to handle money.

Since most people didn't learn about financial skills in school, you can still learn them now. Here are some of the Money management skills that you can follow to improve your skills.

Set a Budget

Track how you spend your money. Do you spend on food, movies, entertainment, and clothes? Do you frequently have an overdraw of your bank account? If this is true, then set a budget. Check your bank statements and note down how much is your expenditure categorically. You will find out how much wastage of money you are not aware of.

Spend wisely

Have a shopping list when you go to the grocery store? Do you first check the price of an item before putting the item in your basket? Use coupons if available. Use online resources and mobile apps to stay focused on your expenditure.

Monitor your spending! By not being attentive to these small tips, you will keep on losing money. It takes time to get coupons, and It takes some effort to find coupons and writing a shopping list and checking the price of an item before buying, it will all be worth it in the long run.

Balance your books

Most people rely on going online to look at their bank balance. By doing this, you won't be able to know how much you are spending at the moment. The best advice is to be accountable by recording all your expenses; you will have avoided over-spending.

Set a plan

You must have a plan for you to accomplish anything. For you to go from location A to B, it won't be possible without a GPS to show the routes. You will end up driving aimlessly going nowhere.

This is similar to not having a financial plan. You will always be broke and not knowing where your money is spent on. "Where did that money go?" With a great plan, you will be able to track your money and expenditure.

Think like an investor

The education system does not teach about handling money, mainly how to invest in growing your wealth. The rich people did not just save $500 a month; they learned how to grow their savings and invest. Turning that $500 into $1000, then into $10,000 and eventually into $100,000 and more.

By investing and growing your money, you will have secured a stable financial future. Think like an investor, and see your money grow.

Have the same financial goals with your partner/spouse

If you're married and you have a joint bank account, then learn to work together. You must both agree with the financial goals.

Make a budget and also see a financial adviser to learn how to invest your money. You must ensure that you have the same financial goals and stay focused.

Save Money

Have a strong commitment to saving your money and securing your future. You can improve your financial situation and make it better! But you need to start with the decision to do so. Make a decision to start saving your money and improving your management skills.

Importance of Money Management

Sticking to a budget and living within your means – is proper money management. Look for great price bargains and avoiding bad deals when purchasing. When you start earning more money, understanding how to invest will become an essential way of reaching your goals like having down payment for a home. Understanding the importance of excellent money management will help you achieve your plans and future goals. Some of the importance of Money Management are:

Better Financial Security

Being cautious of your expenditures and saving, you will be able to save enough for the future. Saving will give you financial security to deal with any unexpected expenses or emergencies like loss of employment, your car breaking down or even saving for a holiday. Having savings, you will not have to use a Credit card to settle crises. Saving is a crucial part of money employment as it helps you build your financial security for a secured future.

Take Advantage of Opportunities

You may encounter opportunities to invest in a business to make more money or an exciting experience like a good deal on a holiday vacation. A friend may inform you of a great investment opportunity or get a great once-in-a-lifetime dream holiday vacation. It can be frustrating not having the money to jump right to these opportunities.

Pay Lower Interest Rates

With excellent money management skills, you can determine your credit score. The highest score means you pay your bills on time and with low-level total debt. Having a higher credit score, you can save more of what you have and have a lower interest rate for car loans, mortgages, credit cards, and even car insurance. And there is the chance to brag to your friends about your high credit score at the parties.

Reduce Stress and Conflict

Paying your bills on time can have a relieving feeling. But on the other hand, being late in paying your bills cause stress and have a negative impact like shutdown in your gas and water supply. Always being broke before your next paycheck can bring conflict and, a significant amount of stress for, couple. And, as we all know, stress brings health problems, experts say, like hypertension, insomnia, and migraines. Being aware of how you can manage your finances, so you have extra cash and savings can put your mind at ease. You will enjoy a stress-free life.

Earn More Money

With your income growing, your financial planning will not only include budgeting for monthly expenses but also figuring out where to invest the extra cash that has accumulated. Knowing different kinds of investments for example stocks and mutual funds, you can earn more money from the investments than what you could have made by leaving the money in your savings account in your bank. But be aware not all investments are recognized as a good investment idea, for example, offshore casinos. One of the best benefits of having investments, you can be at work earning monthly income, and your investments, on the other hand, are making more money for you.

More saving and time

Excellent money management can assist in avoiding your finances from spiraling out of control. It is easy to be in debt if you are unaware of how all your income it's spent monthly. Effective money management means better use of your spare time. You can spend time with your family and friends, by having a clear budget, you will be able to plan for fun days out as you will have available cash to do so.

Peace of mind

Excellent money management gives you some level of calm and peace of mind. With your income and the savings, you can handle any financial demands with the confidence that you have the resources to handle any need that will arise.

Best Money Managers

When developing your investment strategy, you will find yourself seeking some assistance. A well-chosen money manager can help you achieve your financial goals. Research is vital, find the right money manager who will be the perfect fit for your financial goals. There is a lot of information you can get to be able to find a money manager. You can rely on referrals, the internet, or financial companies to get the right money manager for you. In this segment we will go through what a money manager is. How does it work? What is the difference between a money manager and a financial advisor? What is the role of a money manager? What are the pros and cons of having a money manager? And what are the fees required?

Who is a Money Manager?

A money manager, also known as investment managers or portfolio managers. It's an individual or a firm which manages investments portfolio and provide personalized financial advice to an individual or institutional investor. Money managers offer advice to clients about the steps they should take to increase their returns.

How does it work?

Money managers earn a fee for their services and not a commission. In some cases, a client will pay a percentage of the managed assets to their money manager. In this way, both the client and the money manager will work hard towards the success of the portfolio. Here is an example illustrating how money managers work:

Suppose Mary has $20,000 and she wants to invest the money. She will find a money manager to manage her new portfolio. Then she schedules a meeting with the money manager. The money manager inquires about Mary's investment goals, the risk if the investment is a short-term or long-term, etc. Based on Mary's feedback, the money manager will choose a set of securities that will help Mary achieve her financial goals. The money manager will monitor Mary's portfolio on a monthly fee basis, the performance and the value of the portfolio.

What's the difference between a money manager and a financial advisor?

When it comes to your finances, doing it alone can be intimidating as you try to understand the game plan. You need to find the right professional to assist you in meeting your goals.

A financial advisor and a money manager have a lot in common, the two jobs are different, and they can't be handled by one person. A financial advisor is also known as wealth managers. A financial advisor understands the specifics of the client's economic life and creates a detailed investment plan, that is is also known to help the client meet their financial goals. A money manager focuses on managing the strategy your portfolio is invested in.

The role of a money manager:

A good money manager focuses on successfully managing your portfolio strategies, and should be able to meet the following expectations:

√ To consistently manage investments portfolio with their stated investment objectives

√ Appropriate risk management

√ Avoid unnecessary turnover within the management team

√ Operate transparently

What are the pros and cons of having a money manager?

When you have a financial goal, you want it to be a success. One of the ways to achieve that is by getting an expert to help you achieve your goals. Do you have some savings which you are thinking of investing? Then you need a money manager for you to achieve your goals of investing. You need a trustworthy and focused money manager. Consider a lot of things before hiring one. To be able to make the right choice, here are some of the pro and cons of having a money manager:

The pros:

Your money manager knows the financial environment
Your money manager can assist you in constructing an income statement and help you understand the market competition. With a great money manager, you can get an excellent customized financial plan and gain essential insights that will help you in your journey.

Your financial manager will make sure your money financial wisely

If there ever a time that you needed to make sure that your cash made the most significant impact, it's now. With a strained economy, there is no room for errors. Your money manager will assist you to avoid the risks and make sure your money it's spent in a way that will bring the best returns. Wondering whether to expand? If you are also thinking of increasing your investment, a money manager makes the smartest and best-informed decisions and assist you with any questions that you might have.

A money manager will free up your time to do what's most important

Your money manager will take away the stress of financial oversight, and this allows you to focus on other vital parts of life.

Your money manager can help your business function well

If you run a business, the money manager can help you with your business. To find out why invoices taking too long without getting paid, why your business is losing cash, and you are not sure where the wastage is happening. The money manager can implement control measures that allow you to easily track your money movement.

The cons:

Your money manager could be expensive

The main reason for not hiring a money manager is the cost! Your concern is a valid one. Money managers are highly qualified and experienced and usually request higher charges. Who can afford an expensive money manager when you have come a long way without him or her up to this point? The solution here is to do your research to get an affordable money manager who will give you the best quality results as well.

Performance Not Guaranteed

Although your money is managed professionally by the money manager, there are still no guarantees. In a bad market day, even the best money manager may lose money.

Lack of Control

You might not have the time or the knowledge to wisely invest your money; it will not be 100% comforting to some people to hand over control of their money to a stranger.

What is a Money Management Rule?

Investing doesn't necessarily need you to be an expert in the field. As a matter of fact, you don't need to be rich to begin investing. However, most people fail to manage their money because they don't know where to start. Here are some of the rules of money management to guide you through your journey:

- Have a plan

How much are you planning to invest? When do you want to invest? When do you plan to exit? You can start from the end and determine how much money you need to invest. Plan for the future, towards financial freedom.

- Time is money

The earlier you start investing, the better advantage you will have. Time is the biggest asset you have. For every time you invest include retirement savings too. There isn't anything that can make up for the effect of compound interest. If you end up losing money in the market, there is enough time for you to recover when you need it. For example, if you invest $1k for five years, you can make equal to $1.8k or $2k in 6 years, assuming the rate of return is the same. It amounts to a 10% difference if you invest one year later.

Do you sincerely think the 10% difference is worth falling off your investment? Never use the "it's too early to start investing" phrase as an excuse to keep your money under the mattress. It's much better to begin late than never.

- It's emotional

We usually make most of our money decisions emotionally like greed, nervousness, and fear. To be able to focus on your long-term investment plan, do not check your account on a daily basis. There are regular fluctuations in the market and individual stocks. If to are making long-term investments, you don't need the stress of constant checking.

A lot of investors get fear after checking the media, and they end up buying or selling their investments at the wrong time. To avoid making such a mistake, be ready, and try to stay calm.

- Financial Goals

Set short term and long term financial goals. Grow your goals and adjust them monthly. Correct your failures and enjoy the success.

- Save Money

Saving for regular expenses like home maintenance and car expenses. It's advisable to save 5-1o percent of the net income. Save 3 to 6 months of your income to an emergency fund.

- Financial Status

Set different expenses and include your debt payments too. Compare the amount of money coming in and what's going out. Know your debts and net income.

- Set a Budget

Budget and closely monitor your spending plan.

- Record Expenditure

Carefully monitor your money. You can note down and adjust appropriately.

- Know the Difference Between Needs and Wants

To quickly know the difference, a need is something that is required for survival. For example, food, shelter, clothes, and water while a want is everything else. Wants to make life a little bit enjoyable. Put more fused on Needs first. And spend on the Wants only after you have taken care of your needs.

- Use Credit Sensibly

Consider credit for planned purchases only. Take the amount that you can comfortably afford to purchase on credit. Credit payments shouldn't exceed 20% of net pay. Don't borrow from a creditor to settle debt to another creditor.

- Settle your bills on time

Keep a higher credit score. Talk to your creditors in advance to explain your situation, if you won't be paying your bills on time.

Tips Used for Money Management

Money management is a delicate topic. For most individuals, it can be overwhelming and intimidating. You may have retirement savings, or not having enough emergency savings. Whatever your concern is, having a good handle of your finances is the best option. Here are some money management tips to get you started.

Manage Monthly Pay

Know your monthly income to better manage your money. Monthly budget, including rent or mortgage payments, gas bills, and other expenses like student loan payments, can be stressful to keep track of. However, making small changes can help you reduce your debts and expenses. Add extra into your monthly payments. Another advice is to increase payments over a year, or another option is to sign up for an automatic payment program. This will assist you to save time and money every month, as payments are deducted automatically from your savings account.

Track Your Spending Habits

Play detective with your finances. You will need to check the financial status by yourself. It might be overwhelming by limiting yourself to monthly expenses. Check out credit card statements, utilities bank account statements and also electronic payment records. Create a spreadsheet or use a pen and paper and track your expenses.

You can also categories your expenses. For example, labeling purchases as Needs wants savings and debts. You can be more detailed and categories like transport, food, and clothing. It all depends on an individual, how much weeds you want to get. After you have compiled everything in one list, get the total of every category to see how you spend. You will be shocked by the amount of money you spend on a particular expenditure.

- Design a budget

When you track your spending, it will naturally lead to the next step: creating a budget. With the numbers you have from tracking your spending, you can now decide how much money you want to go into each item in your budget. You can also scale back some areas of your expenses that you discover you're overspending. You can write a budget as detailed as you like. Everybody's budget is different. Keep the budget relatively simple.

For proper budgeting, guideline uses the 50/30/20 rule — a strategy to help you divide and allocate your monthly income. The fifty percent will go towards fixed costs example, mortgage or rent, taxes, debt and car payments. The thirty percent will go towards spending, for example, vacation and eating out. And the 20% should go towards savings including emergency fund or investing. Regularly monitor your budget. It's better to start with a basic budget than not having a budget at all. Always save more than you're spending.

- Set Financial Goals

Once you have attained your emergency savings account, you should work towards establishing financial goals. The financial goals can be short term goals such as holiday and long term goals such as saving for college, a house or a retirement plan. The mistakes most people make with their budget is they're short-sighted. Have a long term focus, have a five or ten-year plan. For example, it's easy to get money and buy that fancy car but, you can easily forget that you have a long term plan to have kids, and this can bring new expenses. Try to anticipate those long term goals and how to achieve them.

- Set an Emergency Fund

You never know what the future will be. You could be unemployed or get an emergency. Whether you like it or not, life happens. Your emergency funding will be determined by your budget. Most financial expert's advice is saving 3 to 6 months' worth of expenses. Having an emergency fund to handle unplanned problem will help you feel more secured and prepared. Take away stressful emergencies with a financial cushion. Put your emergency fund in a savings account that is liquid and accessible, but only to be used for emergencies.

Apps Used for Money Management

Times are tough. Whether you earn a high net income or you get by, monitoring where your money is spent. There are many ways to track your spending, how you invest and more. We use our cell phones daily, and we always have our phones in our pockets all the time, using apps to help you manage your money is the best option.

Having a good understanding of your cash flow is very vital in managing your finances. How much of your income is coming in? When does the money get to your bank account? How do you spend the money? These are essential aspects of your financial success. Fortunately, there are a lot of money management apps in the market designed to help you check your bank balance, track your expenditure and, analyze your spending habits. Plus, there are apps that will assist you in making better financial decisions based on the data from your accounts.

And the best part? You can access your financial situation on the go. A lot of these money management apps can be checked online and also on your mobile device. It's very convenient as you can take care of your finances no matter where you are.

What do budget apps do? There are two main types of budget apps. One is an expense tracker — it best-fit people who deduct a lot of items from their taxes. For example, business owners who travel a lot, people who track their meals, transportation, and, all other professions who use expenses trackers. This app will help you track how much money you spend. You also have all the info you need when tax season rears its ugly head. The other type of budget app is the one which helps you track your bank budget, expenses bills, and utilities. These help you track your money, especially for people who manage multiple accounts and pays bills online.

Here are some of the best money management apps you should consider:

- Personal Capital

Personal Capital has excellent features to track your budget and also include information about your investment accounts. And you can easily view on tablets, laptops, desktops and your mobile. It also shows graphs of your investments, that are easy to read and track down your investment performance.

- Mint

Mint is one of the popular budgeting apps. Mint offer features like access to your investment accounts and budgeting tools. The budgeting portion is the main feature, and the investing part is little like an afterthought. The best app if you want to keep a very detailed budget. Mint also has a reminder feature to when your bills are due, and you can also pay your bills from the app.

- Acorns

Acorns take virtual change out of your account. Instead of saving it, the app invests the difference. The app helps you start investing with virtually no effort. You can use Acorns on your transactions. The app has a new shopping type function, Found Money.

- YNAB

YNAB is an acronym for You Need a Budget. YNAB cost $6.99 per month, but they waive the first month's fee. The philosophy for YNAB is " a job for every dollar." YNAB also offers a bank syncing and support feature. YNAB can also help you set your financial goals and make the most of each dollar earned.

- Honeydue

Many couples use spreadsheets to manage their household finances. Honeydue is the best app for couples as it helps couples best co-manage their money. Honeydue helps to track shared bills; the pair can see their accounts in one spot, comment on the transactions, and build bigger and better financial goals. Honeydue has the main feature; couples can decide on how much they can share information with their significant others. This feature helps them to remain focused on their goals and not get caught in the weeds, arguing over the small stuff.

- PocketGuard

PocketGuard will help you find savings in your spending. This app sync with your accounts and enables you to track and analyze your spending, which you can use that data to help you build an excellent budget. You can identify a pattern in your monthly spending, track your bills, and save some money.

- Dollarbird

Dollarbird is an app that assists people who have issues with budgeting. This is a free app; however, it has premium add-ons. Your budget is put in a calendar form, and you can view any upcoming expenses. Other features are, you can color code transactions by category and pay you bills through the recurring transaction. Dollarbird lets you see the projected balance, so you are aware of how much money you can safely spend. The limitation that comes with this app is that the app does not sync with your bank account. With this app, you can quickly enter your transactions manually, and this means you will be more involved with the approach to your money.

- Credit Karma

Credit Karma offers you access to your Credit Report. There are several uses of this app, for example, a company can use the app to determine whether to employ you or to estimate your credit score so as a business can be able to figure out the rates that they will charge you. This app can also be used to determine your loan applications and credit cards. Credit Karma is free to users however, the app earns money by offering targeted ads based on your credit score.

Chapter 9   Dos and Don'ts

Now let's distil the information above into more digestible bites. These tips will be your guideposts along the path to success, and light the way so you avoid the pitfalls new investors are susceptible to.

Seven Tips For Always

1. Don't let your emotions get the best of you.

You have a wealth of information at your fingertips, and now you have the wherewithal to turn all that info into actionable steps. Don't let pride, or wanting to be right, or fear derail you.

2. Trust Yourself

This is the key difference between an okay trader and a great one. It might seem like this contradicts the previous piece of advice, but if you've done your homework and come to a fact-based conclusion, don't let the opinions of others turn you from the path you've decided on.

3. Don't Worry About What's "Hot"

This builds on Tip 2. When you get into the world of investing you'll be getting tips left and right from people who may or may not have an ulterior motive, and almost certainly won't have as much insight into your particular needs as you do. It's easy to let excitement carry you along, but it's almost always dangerous. If you're hearing that a stock is "hot" at a dinner party everyone already knows about it, and it's probably overvalued by this point.

4. Remember Context

Investing doesn't happen in a vacuum. When you hear horror stories about someone losing their house in bad trades, it's always because they forgot about the context of their life. You have to have income that pays the bills and forgetting that to chase the next big windfall is just another emotional mistake that you must avoid.

5. Never. Stop. Diversifying.

Diversification isn't a one-time process. As you sell off parts of your portfolio, you'll reinvest that money in other ways. Make sure your portfolio remains diverse.

6. Be Patient

Making money on the stock market takes a cool head and a steady hand. If you jump out of the water every time it gets a little warm you don't stand a chance. You'll take losses, but you now know how to deal with them. Don't let a small loss become a drain on your assets or on your focus.

7. Respect The Time Limitations of Your Investments

Say you invest in a fund or bond that requires you to hold it for a specified amount of time. During this time, the market spikes, and you realize you'd still make a little bit of money if you sell now and pay the fee for exiting early. While you didn't lose anything in this transaction overall, you've lost the opportunity for that money to make as much as it could have if properly invested. If you know you'll need cash to hand during the time an investment requires, pick a different investment.

Seven Tips For Never

1. Over-Diversification

After all this time drilling the importance of diversification into your head, this may come as a surprise. It's true, though, that there is a thing as too much diversification. If you only have a small amount to invest, and you spread that too thin, you're only leaving yourself the option of buying extremely inexpensive stock. This may cause you to miss opportunities you wouldn't otherwise. In this case, the advice should be: Diversify Wisely.

2. Ignore Fees At Your Own Peril

Even with a discount broker, trades aren't free. Remember to calculate the fees into the price of stocks you buy and to subtract them from your profits on stocks you sell. It seems obvious, but you can trade yourself out into a hole if you're not careful to monitor how much of your money is going to fees and commissions.

3. Don't Think In Dollars

You must think in percentages. For a simple illustration of why, imagine this scenario: You hold 10 shares each of Stock X and Stock Y. Stock X, you bought for $100 per share and it's gone up to $110 in the first quarter you own it. You paid $6 per share for Stock Y, and now it's gone up to $9. While obviously Stock X has gone up $10 and Stock Y has only gone up $3, Stock X has increased 10% while Stock Y has skyrocketed up by 33%. That's quite a difference. Looking at percentages ensures that you're making your money work for you as hard as you can.

4. Analysis Paralysis

You can't noodle over forms and charts forever. At some point, you have to pull the trigger and enter the marketplace. Do your homework, but make sure you get to the real work once that's done.

5. Paying Someone Else To Do Your Job

You've obviously come this far, so you are willing to do the work of investing yourself. Don't pay a full-service broker or advisor to make decisions you can make yourself. Not only is this a waste of money, it removes your ability to use your special knowledge to choose stocks and investments that you believe in.

6. Stay Off The Style Merry-Go-Round

If your goals are lofty and your risk tolerance high, jump in with both feet. If you're a less aggressive investor and want to build a safe "buy and hold" portfolio, choose cautious investments from Day One. Part of learning to be successful on the stock market is practice. You'll need to get used to the swing of the market, and you won't do that if your style is jumping around erratically.

7. Don't Use Real Money Your First Time Out!

There are many sites that offer "virtual stock markets" that will let you get a feel for how buying and selling stocks works without investing a dime. It's absolutely worth your time to spend a few hours on these sites getting your feet wet. Beware, though: this is a particularly easy place to get hung up in your homework, leading to #4: Analysis Paralysis. A few hours is good, but a few hours is enough.

Obviously, there is a lot more depth in some of these areas, but you are now well rooted in a foundation of knowledge that will allow you to get started as in investor. Keep your head clear, focus on facts, and you're well on your way to investing success.

Beginner's Mistakes to Avoid

Playing out of your depth: Scared money never wins.
Fear freezing thinking: Analysis Paralysis

While doing your practice trading, pay close attention to how much your trades vary in profit/loss during each 5-minute segment, how much it varies in 15 minutes, half hour, hour and so on. Don't do this just one day or one hour but over several days or even a couple of weeks. The reason to do this is quite simple: You are, so-to-speak, "testing your risk tolerance." Admittedly, there is a difference between paper trading and using real money. Still it is better that you get this experience than not. If you feel these variations are not acceptable for any reason, this type of trading may not be for you.

It is quite natural for you to have some 'analysis paralysis', especially the moment as you switch to trading real money instead of practice trading. If your brain is overwhelmed so completely with all you are trying to learn, be patient with yourself. Give yourself enough time for your brain to assimilate the process. With practice your thinking and reactions become faster. You will also notice the points at which you start stressing during losing trades; take some notes on this because you need to know how this amount to determine your risk tolerance and experience the point where your decisions are triggered by emotions. By the time you can practice trade and accomplish 25 consecutive "successful" (error free whether winner or loser) trades, you will be able to get some idea of what risk level you can handle.

Using a Blind System and Using Technicals Blindly

By "blind system," I mean those get-rich-quick scams that promise lots of money with very little work, risk, or thought. Buyers beware. No one who would ever sell you such a system will ever agree to pay your losses. Trading blind on promises from unproven sources - is risky territory.

Remember that technical indicators are tools, not foolproof trading systems and must be used in the context of market concepts, trends, and patterns.

Impatience and Not Preparing Well Enough

Think of trading as owning your own business. You invest a few bucks for information and supplies, then a research period to test feasibility as best you can, and then risk your hard-earned money. In an earlier chapter, I strongly suggested you practice trade with a ledger, keeping notes, until you can string together 25 consecutive trades with no errors. It can take a while to do this successfully. Be patient and take time to learn by doing, not just reading about it. Remember no two traders are identical; find what works for you.

Ignore Brain Pattern Dominance

When you trade using technical charting and indicators, you will notice that you start to "see" a lot of potential patterns that can be forming. This is apophenia; your brain working hard to find patterns and project outcomes. This is normal. Wait and let the "market tell you" what is going on, and don't allow your attention to stray when your brain sends you all the possible outcomes of things that are not yet in your charts and indicators. Until you gain some experience, this is one of the most difficult things to learn. Trading with technical indicators and charts is not a perfect science by any means. The indicators will sometimes lead you astray no matter how long you study them. It is quite common for inexperienced traders to think that if only they find the right technical indicators, they will win the vast majority of trades. This is a very popular myth. It is something almost everyone wants to believe.

It is a rookie mistake to think that just because you got a good night's sleep, got up early, read the day's financial news or financial channel, and have spent hours of practice - that the market will send you a perfect technical indicator trade in the first ten minutes of your trading. You must have patience. Sometimes, you see a trade instantly. Other times you can go more than an hour and see no chances at all. Other days, you'll have almost too many good signals. These things do not happen on a schedule. You will see some days that are volatile and fast, maybe too fast for your risk tolerance. Other days will be so slow, you might feel bored and that you've wasted time. Over time, you learn to recognize those time periods - when trying to trade at all is impossible; so don't. Some days as the saying goes, "You get all dressed up and there is just no place to go." Hope is not a strategy. Let the market tell YOU what's happening, not the other way around.

Over-using Genius of Hindsight

This is another of the "most common" mistakes new and veteran traders make. I've already written extensively about this. You can learn from genius of hindsight, but you should never judge your ability to trade with information you did not have during the trade. This may seem counter-intuitive so I want to be perfectly clear about this: You can LEARN from hindsight; it can be a debriefing. Recognize that judging your decisions with hindsight is always a hypothetical matter, never based on the same facts you had before or during a trade.

Trying to Guess Reversals

There are times when you may have a strong bias about what the market "should" do. For example: The market may have extended time periods of remarkable gains or losses. You come to feel the market should be ready for some reaction, retracement, or some adjustment. Times like this will give you a strong bias and it is too easy to forget that you could be considering trading on that bias, even though the technical indicators or other market action is telling you otherwise. Over time, you will learn to use your technical charts and indicators much like a night aircraft pilot uses instruments to navigate. It is quite common to 'over read' your indicators like the MACD. By that, I mean you will naturally start to anticipate what might happen next and trade on this speculation, rather than waiting for a more reliable signal. As discussed often in this book, humans have a very strong predilection to find patterns where they do not really exist. To allow yourself to follow this inclination is to run the extra risk of ignoring your charting and indicators. Avoiding this mistake, takes an enormous amount of patience and a bit of experience.

Letting recent experience skew your thinking

So what does "your recent experience" really mean? To a stock trader, it could mean last year or last month. To a day-trader, it could mean 15 minutes ago, yesterday, or two hours ago or even five-minutes ago. When a day trader has a string of consecutive losses, it can result in the trader being less aggressive and overly cautious. This can materialize into a reaction of: a) taking profits too quickly to "make up" for the losing trades, b) perhaps letting the losses accumulate due to being hopeful, or c) exiting a trade in a small drawdown too quickly to avoid more losses. Any of these three reactions as a result of recent losing trades can be directly categorized as letting your emotions influence your trading decisions.

The solution to this problem is learn to rely on the experience you gain using the candlesticks and MACD. Over time, you will gain more confidence in your ability to read market news, to be aware of scheduled reports and major events that occur during a trading day and will better understand how to interpret the various intensities of trading signals. As you gain experience with reading candlesticks and using the MACD indicator – you will learn to rely more on these things – than to listen to that voice in your head that brings emotional reactions as well as its ability to find patterns that are really not there, those optical illusions due to apophenia and pareidolia. Each trade you make is no more related the last trade than is one coin toss that follows another. They are mutually exclusive even though your brain is hard-wired to relate them. This first step in avoiding this is to be aware of it.

Not Evaluating Your Trading as a Business Plan

You must keep a clear and accurate trading log. You'll be using it to evaluate your methods and results. It will be the equivalent of a business ledger that records expenses (losses) and profits and it will detail your methods. It is easily possible to over-think everything. The ledger you keep will show you truthful results and it can be used to identify both mistakes and to help find improvements you can make. At the end of the day, you will be your own business manager and can inspect your books to see how your business is doing. Your account balance won't lie, it will tell you if you are doing things right.

There is No Such Thing as a Winning Streak

There is a certain amount of euphoria when you make money trading. There is always a temptation to think you are on a roll, but this is only an illusion. Each of your trades must justify its own risk-reward.

Chapter 10 Managing Risk in Trading and the Role of Journaling

The first thing you need to know as a trader is that you will run volumes of trades and experience a lot of risks. Trading the markets is one of the riskiest investment techniques, and many people go for day trading because they have the potential for higher gains over a short period. If you have a small account, day trading gives you the chance to grow small accounts in such a short timeframe.

Risk comes about because you have to execute hundreds of trades in such a short time. You also have the capacity to place any trade you want, for as low as $500 or as high as $25,000 in a single trade. The trades are also at high speed, which means the market can swing any way – up or down. The direction of the market determines whether you make a loss or a profit.

Day trading gives you two realms of strategies to go with – high risk trading strategies or Lowe risk strategies. The goal of a successful trader is to maximize profit while lowering risks. Every time you place a trade, you need to evaluate the risk of the trade and then weight it against the potential reward. Often times this is made worse by our emotional reaction to various price directions. For instance, since you experienced a loss recently, the next logical step would be to take a higher risk on the next trade so that you can compensate on the loss. Experienced traders have a heightened level of awareness that they use to recognize a loss and reward and will make sure they take the right decision. However, you have to learn the skill over time.

You can develop a sense of decision making by keeping a journal as you trade and then reviewing the notes after the close of the market.

Different Types of risk

When talking about risk, you need to consider the different types in order for you to understand what we are saying. As a day trader, your primary role is to know the distance between the entry and the stop. Stop loss needs to be based on a resistance area on the chart or recent support.

Majority of your losses need to happen when a trade hits the stop price. This means you won't make any profit on whatever you are trading.

The second type of risk id the volatility of the market. As day traders, volatility is a friend to all of us, but it is also risky because markets that are extremely volatile tend to result in higher losses than what you actually planned for. Since there is a sense of inherent risk in trading, you need to try and avoid placing a trade when the volatility cannot be predicted, for instance when there is breaking news.

The other type of risk is exposure risk. Exposure results when you multiply the price of shares by the number of held shares. As an investor, you increase this risk when you hold on positions for a very long time. To mitigate this risk, you need to hold onto shares for a short time.

If you are holding onto large positions for a long time you stand to experience stock halts. Halts can take hours or days, though they are rare. The most common halts are those waiting for the release of news or volatility halts. Anytime a stock halts, it can lead to a different price. The biggest risk is that the stock might reopen at a very different price, which might be lower than the current price of the stock. You can take steps to reduce the effect of the halts by understanding what leads to the halts in the first place.

Journaling

If you are looking at a routine that is easy to implement and that can change the way you trade, then think about keeping a journal. The journal is a little black book that details what you do each day.

The aim of keeping a journal is to help improve your setups so that you use your experiences to analyze and help refine your trading while you improve the whole experience.

Here, we look at all you need to come up with a journal and maintain it.

What is A Journal?

A trading journal is a way to keep track of what you are doing o daily basis as a day trader. You jot down notes of what you do each day especially the different trades (or lack of) and the results of any action you take.

The trading journal needs to be tailored to your trading styles and preferences. You can keep the journal in a physical notebook or a detailed digital document on your computer. Regardless of the format, when maintained with due diligence, the trading journal can be the best way to make you a better day trader.

How Does the Trading Journal Help You Achieve Better Trades?

There are a number of ways in which a trading journal will help you become better at what you do.

Many traders attribute their success to creating and maintaining a trading journal. By noting down the different trades, you are able to check the progress over time. This allows you to find out what is working or not and change or modify them to succeed.

Helps You develop discipline in Trading

Having a trading journal helps you develop discipline as you trade. How does it do so? Well, it forces you to follow the guidelines that you have set down.

The sense of accountability that you get when you have a trading journal makes sure you are responsible for research and trading. If you know what you need to keep a log each day, you do it without fail. Making sure you log your trades and whatever happens requires a lot of discipline. Good habits such as these require you to go straight when executing trades.

Helps You Master Your Emotions

One of the top suggestions to help you run trades the right way is to trade like you are not human. Machines do not have emotions and approach all the processes in a scientific way.

However, this is easier said than done. When you get in a position to lose money, usually you find it tough getting emotion out of the way.

Keeping a journal can help you keep the emotions out of the way. With a journal in place, you get to keep track of how you feel emotionally in various trading stages. This is just to keep the emotions in check.

With time, you realize that there is a pattern that is emerging, for instance, you might find yourself getting calmer and taking orders the right way each time.

Improves Your Risk Management Practices

Day trading comes with a high level of risk. This is something that you cannot change at all because it is the nature of the market for things to run this way. However, there are various ways in which you can mitigate these risks. For one, you need to invest a large amount of research and study to give you the knowledge that you need to choose the least risky trades possible.

With a journal, you can learn things about risk tolerance. For instance, you might find that you have consistently been able to hold positions for longer and you have been losing profits as a result. You might also find that you have issues getting out of trades because you have been taking positions that are too big for your stage.

By looking at the risks that you have been taking and how they affect the results you return, you get to make adjustments.

For instance, you might exit trades sooner or you might end up taking smaller positions based on the results you return. This way you help reduce risks and improve risk management.

Creating the Perfect Trading Diary

Now that you know how effective the trading journal is, you need to know how to come up with the best one. Here are a few tips for success when coming up with a journal:

- Be consistent

Trading needs you to have a routine. You will probably get the most out of the journal if you have a routine that you follow religiously.

You also need to follow the routine to the latter. This means that you are consistent with what you do day in day out. For instance, you need to wake up early each day to prepare for trading. This allows you to get errands and tasks out of the way early and gives you to do research so that you are ready to roll when the market starts.

This is a directive though because since many traders are doing other responsibilities, you need to come up with the right schedule that works for you. Choose the routine that will work for you and that you can stick to easily.

- Analyze the Market

The more the trades that you track, the more data you have to deal with and the more you get to learn and the faster you do it.

By recording the trades, overall thoughts, market observations and more, you aren't just learning from the mistakes that you are doing, but you are also gaining a sense of how to perform the right market analysis.

For instance, with the right trading data, you get to notice gains and losses in a particular industry or sector. This can give you clues on the trends in the market that you might have missed out.

Once you see what is working and what isn't, you get to have a targeted market analysis.

- Analyze and Come Up with Your Own Setups

A trading journal allows you to come up with the right setups. Here is how this works out:

- Find the setups that trigger trade entry

When do you enter the market? The trading journal helps you figure everything out. You need to go into each trade with a plan. However, if you realize that you are entering trades too soon or too late based on the journal, you can then decide to try something different.

With the perfect trading journal, you have the capacity to determine the setups that trigger the entries.

- Gain Insight into the Market

When you record your own setups, you have the ability to gain insight into the market that you are trading in. you get to notice market trends and how they might end up affecting the setups.

As a trader, understanding the way the market runs is ideal because it helps you to keep up to date. The market is dynamic, and the setups that work in one market condition might not work for other conditions. When you understand the market, you get to navigate around and acclimatize to new markets.

- Know the Appropriate Lot Size

In any market, the lot size means the number of shares which you buy in any transaction. The theory of size allows you to regulate price quotes. It is basically the size of the trade that you place in the financial market.

With price regulation being a part of every market, you need to always be aware of the number of units that you purchase eon contract, and determine the price you pay per unit.

Make sure you keep track of the lot sizes that you deal with in any trade, as it helps you to decide the types of approaches that you take in the future.

- Determine the Style of Trading

Many traders choose to be one type of trader or another. Many of them do it by force, which is a fact that isn't the best. As a trader, you need to naturally gravitate towards a specific trading style, and not force it.

Rather than chasing after what is trendy or what you have seen other traders do, it is advisable to focus on a style of trading that gives you profit, whether you go after long or short positions.

A trading journal can help you determine the type of trade that is best suited for you by giving you a summary of the trades that gave you money.

- Understand Profit Placement

Trading is a probability game, with so many moving pieces that make it work. With so many parts that are needed to make everything work, you need to make sure you get everything right the first time. This isn't easy at all.

Here are a few specifics that you need to master:

- Cut losses fast: you need to learn to cut losses quickly, which means you pull out of a position earlier than later, even if it means missing out on a few profits. It is always good to be safe than sorry. Having a trading journal helps you determine when to get out of a trade. If you notice that you are losing constantly, then journaling can help you learn how to cut losses fast. Additionally, if you notice that you are getting out of trades too early, then you can start staying gin the game a little bit longer.
- Stop losses: you need to learn how to come up with the best stop loss order. The order can help you release the order when you reach a particular price. With the right stop loss order, you can buy the security rather than selling it when you reach a certain price. Make sure you record the different entry and exit positions; how much you have risked and the results of everything. As the information collects over time, you can determine what your best setups are so that you can focus on replicating the profits you gained in the past to eliminate losses.

Apart from this information, you also need to record other things so that you make the most out of each entry:

- The date: this shouldn't be left out of the journal. Not only does it help you to track what you were doing and when you were doing it, but it allows you to go back and look at the performance of the stock on that date in future. Never assume that you will rack everything in your brain!
- The Time Frame: do not just record the date, but make sure you know the perfect time for each entry. In the world of trading, minutes matter. Trading in the morning can make a huge difference compared to trading in the afternoon. For instance, the setup that works for you during the morning hours might not work the same way in the afternoon.
- Price in: this is the point where the journal starts working well with the trading plan. When coming up with a trading plan, you set the key tactics such as the entry point, the exit and what you plan to gain from this trade. This helps you to stick to the plan and then keep emotions out of things. In the journal, make sure you note the price at which you entered a successful trade.

• Price out: don't just mark the time that you entered the trade – also take note of the price that you exit the trade too. The exit is also as vital as the entrance. Keeping this data allows you to analyze whether you are staying in a position for the right amount of time. Note any difficulties that you encounter getting out of the position, as this might affect the level of risk next time.

• Amount you are risking: before you enter a trade, you need to determine the amount of money you plan to put into the trade. Note: The money you put tin should be an amount you can risk losing. So, how much money should you risk on a trade? The answer is that you need to always take a cautious position, and never try to risk what you can't lose. You do not want to enter into a trade and blow up the account as this might trigger emotional trading.

Tips for Creating an Efficient Trading Journal

1. Identify the Patterns That lead to Losses

As a trader, you can't eliminate the risk of making losses. For many traders, the success rate is 70 percent, and many of them know that the 100 percent win rate is a myth.

You can never control how much you win, but you can at least control the amount you can lose by cutting losses fast.

You also get to learn from the losses. Once you have a trading journal, you begin to identify patterns that lead to losses and assess what is happening.

2.   Identify the Patterns That Have Made You Profit

As a trader, you not only focus on the things that went wrong, but also look at what went right as well. You need to chart patterns in the trades to help you analyze what make you the most money. Many successful traders base their success on being able to identify patterns. Many depend on stock charts, but later realize that even the trading journal gives them an insight into what they need to do.

3.   Go for Professional Assistance

Trading classes give you an asset that you will never regret in your trading life. Even with the right data, you might find yourself failing to make profitable trades because you do not have the mechanics to make things work for you. When you take time to learn the mechanics of trading, you find that you have the basis to identify key indicators and add them to the journal.

Just like any other trade, the more you get prepared to execute trades the more successful you become. The knowledge originates from previous traders that have become successful in their efforts.

4. Work With templates

Templates make it easy for you to come up with a plan. There are many platforms online that offer you both paid and free templates that you can use to create the perfect journal, all you need to do is to choose the one that suits you then customize it to your liking. As you become more adept, you find that the journal becomes your best friend, and it also becomes more detailed.

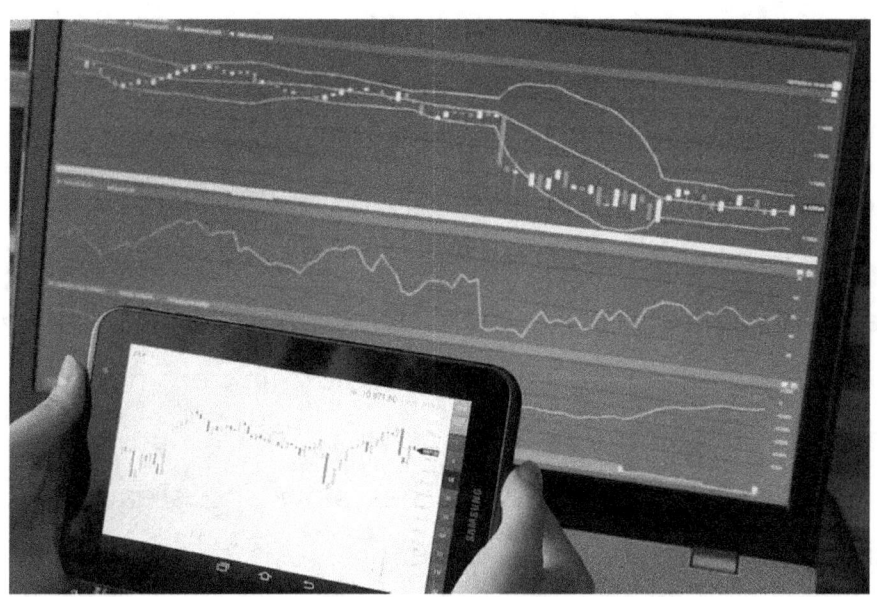

Conclusion

Now that you have made it to the end of this book, you hopefully have an understanding of how to get started day trading forex, as well as a strategy or two, or three, that you are anxious to try for the first time. Before you go ahead and start giving it your all, however, it is important that you have realistic expectations as to the level of success you should expect in the near future.

While it is perfectly true that some people experience serious success right out of the gate, it is an unfortunate fact of life that they are the exception rather than the rule. What this means is that you should expect to experience something of a learning curve, especially when you are first figuring out what works for you. This is perfectly normal, however, and if you persevere you will come out the other side better because of it. Instead of getting your hopes up to an unrealistic degree, you should think of your time spent with the forex market as a marathon rather than a sprint which means that slow and steady will win the race every single time.

This book has been able to give you all the information that you will need to become a successful day trader. We have also given you all the information that you need to avoid the classic mistakes that people make when they attempt to be successful with this. Through this book you will have gained knowledge on the rules and strategies of day trading while making sure that you are being able to be aware of losses and the management of risk. We've also explained the reasons behind why you should be aware of these things in the first place as it is a very important issue.

Loss is a part of this business and it's something that you should recognize and learn about right away so that you know how to avoid these issues and to make smart decisions instead of decisions that are unwise and that can lead you into bad decisions. Because we want you to be able to be successful we explain the rules of taxes and the plans you will need to understand as well. This will ensure you have the best chance of moving forward with the best information possible as well.

We have also given you the best information on the platforms that you can use for trading as well as the many tools at your disposal. There are many different software that you can use and that you can utilize for your benefit. The best part of this is that you can use your computer and get down to business. When you understand the ins and outs of this business you can move through it and past people easily to maximize your own success.

One of the key things that we have taught you in this book is that you need to exercise the art of patience. Being patient with the market, the plans, the people and your marketing and decision making is going to let you have more power financially and more power in this field. You need to make sure that you have the patience to be able to push through and reach your goals. This takes time and work and if you have the patience you will be able to do this successfully.

Remembering that this is a hot commodity in today's society will serve you well as well. When you realize how many people are in this field and how many people are wanting to do the same thing and have a great level of success like you are is going to help you give the motivation you need to push past them and keep moving toward your own success. However, this also gives you a good idea of what you're up against which is an important part of this as well.

If you use the tips and information in this book to your advantage, you will be able to make sure that you can be successful and that you will be able to trade with ease earning yourself the experience and income you desire.

www.ingramcontent.com/pod-product-compliance
Lightning Source LLC
Chambersburg PA
CBHW070632220526

45466CB00001B/160